Albert Frey, Architect

ROSA
Gebhard

Princeton Architectural Press : New York

PUBLISHED BY
Princeton Architectural Press
37 East 7th Street
New York, NY 10003
212.995.9620

For a catalog of books, call 1.800.722.6657.
Visit our website at www.papress.com.

© 1999 Princeton Architectural Press
All rights reserved
Printed and bound in China
02 01 00 99   4 3 2 1

No part of this book may be used or reproduced in any manner without
written permission from the publisher, except in the context of reviews.

Every effort has been made to contact the owners of copyright for the photographs herein.
Any omissions will be corrected in subsequent printings.

EDITING AND BOOK DESIGN: Sara E. Stemen
EDITORIAL ASSISTANCE: Sara Moss

SPECIAL THANKS TO: Ann Alter, Eugenia Bell, Jan Cigliano, Jane Garvie, Caroline Green, Beth Harrison, Clare Jacobson, Mirjana Javornik, Therese Kelly, Leslie Ann Kent, Mark Lamster, Anne Nitschke, Lottchen Shivers, and Jennifer Thompson of Princeton Architectural Press   —Kevin C. Lippert, Publisher

LIBRARY OF CONGRESS CATALOGING-IN-PUBLICATION DATA
Rosa, Joseph
    Albert Frey, architect / Joseph Rosa : introduction by David Gebhard.
      p. cm.
    Originally published: New York, NY : Rizzoli International, 1990.
    Includes bibliographical references and index.
    ISBN 1-56898-205-4 (alk. paper)
    1. Frey, Albert, 1903– —Criticism and interpretation. 2. International style (Architecture)—United States.
I. Title.
NA737.F74R6 1999
720'.92—dc21   99-23419
                                                                                                                          CIP

CONTENTS

Acknowledgments : vii

Introduction, David Gebhard : ix

The Early Years, 1903–30 : 1

Letters between Le Corbusier and Albert Frey : 12

America, The East Coast, 1930–39 : 19

"The Evolution of Architectural Form," Albert Frey : 55

America, The West Coast, 1939–55 : 59

America, The Late West Coast, 1955–86 : 105

Afterword : 137

Building List : 141

Selected bibliography: writings on Albert Frey : 144

Selected bibliography: writings by Albert Frey : 146

Credits : 147

Index : 148

In memory of my mother, Chiara Allocca, and father, Joseph Paul Rosa

ACKNOWLEDGMENTS

OVER THE YEARS that I have conducted research on Albert Frey, there have been many individuals to whom I am indebted for sharing their memories of Frey, their knowledge of the American modern movement, and their encouragement and moral support. Most of all, my deepest gratitude must go to Albert Frey for allowing me into his life. After numerous trips to Palm Springs to meet with Frey and discuss his work, I moved to California for six months and spent almost every weekend with him. His hospitality and generosity were unparalleled.

To Peter D. Eisenman, Charles Gwathmey, Barbara Neski, and Tod Williams, for their support and encouragement from the very start, which enabled me to make this book a reality.

To David Gebhard, Philip Johnson, Esther McCoy, Julius Shulman, Richard Guy Wilson, and Marges Bacon, for sharing their knowledge of Frey's work and the period, which gave me further insight into his work in the context of this period. A special note of gratitude to David Morton, who edited the first edition of this book.

Through numerous interviews and correspondence over the years, I am indebted to Alfred (Seppel) and Jane West Clauss, Hamilton Beatty, Mrs. Louis Benoist, Tim Benton, Irving Bowman, Robson C. Chambers, John Porter Clark, Marion Cooke, Hester Diamond, Craig Ellwood, Percival Goodman, Alastair Gordon, Naomi Sawelson-Gorse, Mrs. Wallace K. Harrison, Mr. and Mrs. Sam Hinton, Elaine S. Jones, Edward A. Killingsworth, Marge Kocher, Sandra Kocher, Pierre Koenig, Ingrid Kristiansen, Trudy Kunt-Frey, Peter Koller, Maxwell Levinson, Richard Longstreth, Jim Louis, Michael Lynch, Dione Neutra, Julian Neski, Victoria Newhouse, Culver Nichols, Alfred Roth, Raphael Soriano, Jon Michael Schwarting, William Storrer, Bill Strauss, E. Stewart Williams, and Gary Wolf, for sharing their personal knowledge.

The research for this book was supported in part by grants from The Graham Foundation for Advanced Studies in the Fine Arts and the National Endowment for the Arts, which afforded me the time and funding necessary to complete this project.

To the various individuals and institutions that assisted me in conducting my research: John E. Ingram, Eileen Parris, Mary Keeling, and Jim Garret of the Colonial Williamsburg Foundation Library, Special Collections, the A. Lawrence Kocher Papers, Williamsburg, Virginia; Evelyne Trehi and Martine Lasson of the Fondation Le Corbusier, Paris; David Hinkle and Kenneth Frampton for sponsoring my Visiting Scholar status (1987–88) at Avery Library, Columbia University, New York; Lauren Bricker at the University of California at Santa Barbara Art Museum Architectural Drawing Collection;

Marla Berns and Phyllis Plous at the University of California at Santa Barbara Art Museum; Janice Lyle at the Palm Springs Desert Museum; Wayne K. Olson of the United States Department of Agriculture, National Agricultural Library, Beltsville, Maryland; Suzanne Sutton of the Palm Springs Public Library; The Richard J. Neutra Archives, Special Collection, University Research Library, University of California, Los Angeles; the Getty Foundation, Santa Monica, California; the New York Public Library; the Museum of Modern Art Library, New York, New York; and the Unified School District of Palm Springs, California.

To my friends and colleagues who have assisted me on various aspects of both editions of this book: Brad Dunning, Steven Forman, Frances Hsu, Stephen Leet, Frank Rotnofsky, Anthony Merchell, Martin Mervel, Michael Rotondi, Brian Reiff, and Susan and Colin Scott, for their valuable support and aid. Sandra Lisa Forman for her translations of Frey's and Le Corbusier's correspondence. Kim Shkapich for designing the previous edition of this book in the spirit of Frey's work. To Bette Frank and Robin Noble for helping me edit the text from the first draft to the final edit, with a special thanks to Robin who has assisted me with the book from its inception.

I would like to thank publisher Kevin Lippert and editor Sara Stemen of Princeton Architectural Press for making this updated edition possible. A special note of thanks to Sara for editing this version of the manuscript and for her elegant design of this edition.

To my wife, Louise, and son, Hugo; sister, Linda; and my late father, for giving me strong, stable, loving support.

Joseph Rosa

INTRODUCTION

A.1　　　　　　　　　　　　A.2　　　　　　　　　　　　A.3

AT THE TIME of Albert Frey's arrival at the California desert community of Palm Springs, in the fall of 1934, this community had assumed its present stance as "...an ultra smart winter resort for movie stars, and for people who like and can afford to live where and as movie stars live...."[1] The project that brought Frey to this remote hideaway for the rich was a small combination apartment and office (the Kocher-Samson Building) that he and A. Lawrence Kocher had designed for Kocher's brother, Dr. J. J. Kocher. In this, his first response to the climate and environs of the desert, Frey provided a concrete, steel, and glass design which strongly asserted the modernist view that a twentieth-century building should in image and fact be a universal machine.

This view, that the machine object should be aloft from the specificity of its environs, was adopted by other architects in Palm Springs in the 1930s. The Los Angeles architects Erle Webster and Adrian Wilson designed in 1936 an extensive hillside house [fig. A.1], which posed as a streamlined ship hovering over the rugged rock outcrops of its site; earlier, in 1933, the Prairie School architect William Gray Purcell (with Evera Van Bailey) had briefly taken over the image of International Style modern for his own Palm Springs retreat [fig. A.2].[2] In the later thirties, the modernist image was insistently carried out in steel and glass in a group of metal-framed and -sheathed vacation houses, produced by Fabricated Houses, Inc. in 1937, and by Richard J. Neutra in his delicately detailed Miller House of 1938 [fig. A.3].

Frey's Kocher-Samson Building, as well as other modernist excursions of the thirties in Palm Springs, pointedly illustrates the high priority that architects and clients have continually placed on imagery. But these modern, up-to-date-appearing machines could cope with the desert and its climate only during the mild winter months, not during the boiling heat of the late spring, summer, or fall. Only with the gradual introduction in the 1930s of refrigerated air conditioning could these machine-image designs really be in fact functional, year-round dwellings.

In his 1939 volume *In Search of a Living Architecture* Frey juxtaposed a pair of photographs, the first showing one of his Palm Springs houses (the Guthrie house of 1935), the other of a traditional adobe building of the Southwest, suggesting that the modernists were looking closely at regional forms when they designed their buildings.[3] The substance of this analogy resided in the realm of form, not in any real similarity of response to the climate and geography of the place. The modernists were not alone in this commitment to form at the expense of responding to and expressing the unique nature of this section of the California desert. By the end of the thirties, the

1 | Federal Writers' Project, WPA, *California: A Guide to the Golden State* (New York: Hastings House, 1939 & 1954), 628.

2 | William Gray Purcell, "Give Yourself a Build-up," *Northwest Architect* 6:2 (1941): 4–7.

3 | Albert Frey, *In Search of a Living Architecture* (New York, Architectural Book Publishing Co., Inc., 1939), 38–39.

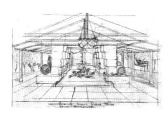

A.4

A.5

close-to-universal image employed in and around Palm Springs was that of the California ranch house, that decade's update of the Spanish colonial revival tradition. The Spanish-Mediterranean had been introduced into the area in the 1920s, and had resulted in an array of impressively designed buildings, ranging from the Moorish towered El Mirador Hotel of 1927 (Walker and Eisen) to Gordon Kaufmann's romantic assemblage of resort buildings, La Quinta, of 1928–29. By 1939 Palm Springs was "…uniformly of California pseudo-Spanish architecture…."[4] While a few of the larger of these buildings were of reinforced concrete, and there were a handful of traditional adobe or native stone, most were thin-walled, wood-stud buildings, sheathed in white cement stucco. These Palm Springs houses and other buildings generally mirrored, in their siting, landscape design, and plans, similar Spanish or Mediterranean-image buildings and houses being built throughout coastal California. Though a palm tree here and there (and an occasional tamarisk) might conjure up a hint that this was the desert, the close-to-universal approach to the landscape was to treat the place as a transformed green oasis.

There were small exceptions to this approach: Arthur Heineman's Davidson house (1927) snuggled itself into the rocky base of the mountains that define the western side of Palm Springs, and John Byers, one of Southern California's principle exponents of the use of adobe, created an environmentally sensitive house and landscape for Julian St. John Noland (1933–34).

The one brief moment when architects sought to respond closely to the unique qualities and climate of Palm Springs was in the early 1920s. It should not be surprising that the most sensitive response came from a designer trained as a landscape architect, Lloyd Wright.[5] His Oasis Hotel (1923–28) employed reinforced concrete to create a visual game between the suggestion of a cool, sheltered cave and the atmosphere of an exotic Arabic tent set on the desert [A.4, Dining Room, 1927]. Another unbuilt design called for digging right into the earth to create the Desert Hacienda (1926); in other instances he oriented rooms of a projected house around a courtyard, which emerged as the living room of the dwelling (1925–26); and in his project for Ellen True (1924), he created a whole resort community of "Rockery tent-houses." Lloyd Wright's Los Angeles colleague R. M. Schindler explored similar approaches in several unbuilt schemes for Palm Springs [A.5, project, House in the Desert, 1924]. In these designs the cold, concrete-enshrouded caves of the dwellings spring open into high-walled, landscaped, pool-oriented courtyards.[6] In Lloyd Wright's and Schindler's designs, the dwellings became, in the end, precise, man-made objects, with the dramatic, unspoiled desert and its sparse vegetation left intact around them.

Frey's response to these early, innovative approaches and to the persistence of traditional Spanish-Mediterranean imagery, coupled with his own involvement in the international modernist scene, was, from the beginning, never single-minded nor doctrinarian. He ended up pursuing at least three distinct paths, and what is remarkable is that these decidedly different paths were generally followed simultaneously.

As a machine-age modernist, Frey created, after World War II, a group of "space-age" buildings, which in their strong expressionist qualities were only paralleled by the pre-World War II designs of Frederick Kiesler, and later by some of the buildings of Bruce Goff and John Lautner. Frey's own house (No. I) in Palm Springs of 1947 and 1953 and his 1958 North Shore Yacht Club on the Salton Sea are two of America's great odes to the romance of the machine. His vision of the machine was not that of the high-art abstractions of Le Corbusier and others, nor that of the everyday-encountered machine. Frey's machine images express a sense of enjoyment, delight, and play more

4 | Federal Writers' Project, WPA, op. cit., 628.

5 | David Gebhard and Harriette Von Breton, *Lloyd Wright, Architect* (Santa Barbara: Art Galleries, University of California, 1971), 14–22.

6 | David Gebhard, *Schindler* (Salt Lake City: Peregrine Smith, Inc., 1980), 51–52.

akin to the popular science fiction of the comic strip than to the world of high-art modernism. The decidedly unique quality of his machine imagery was that he realized it through the use of mundane, everyday products. This meant that the viewer was transported into the science-fiction imagery by proceeding from the known (everyday, cheap machine products) into a vision beyond the normal.

The second direction pursued by Frey was a low-keyed, generally refined modernism—a version of the modern that came to dominate the American architectural scene in the 1950s and 1960s. Much of this work was produced in partnership with John Porter Clark, and later with Robson C. Chambers. The modernist buildings of these partnerships are only distinguishable from hundreds of other similar buildings of the time by their sensitive handling of proportions and details. The Palm Springs City Hall of 1952–57, the 1948–49 Katherine Finchy Elementary School, and other similar designs are in the best sense of the term classics of California post-World War II modernism.

While other modernists, like Richard J. Neutra (in his 1927 *Wie Baut Amerika?*), paid a symbolic homage to vernacular and traditional forms of California and of the Southwest, Frey in contrast looked upon them as legitimate sources for contemporary architecture.[7] Before the Second World War he had noted: "When we still admire and even imitate architecture of the past which has outlived its practical usefulness to us, it is either because the formal composition possesses qualities of abstract beauty, or because we feel for such architecture an emotional attachment, psychologically or historically founded."[8] With this attitude as a background, and with the predilections of many of his conventional middle-class clients in mind, it should not be a surprise to find that much of his work falls loosely within the pre- and post-World War II California ranch house mode. Frey's single-floor, rambling ranch houses, like those of his contemporary Cliff May, illustrate how modern and specific to a time revived historic forms can be.

Frey's own house (No. II) of 1963–64 indicates how he could look back to the early 1920s experiments of Lloyd Wright and Schindler, link these concepts with his own version of the machine image, and couple them with the simplicity of form associated with the California ranch house. This house plays two divergent games simultaneously: it sits within and is passively overpowered by the rock outcropping of the mountainside upon which it has been situated, but nonetheless, through its precisely delineated concrete garage, stairs, walls, and swimming pool terrace, the house asserts the unquestioned primacy of the man-made object.

Perhaps, in a way, Frey's comments pertaining to Boulder Dam on the Colorado River sum up what he sought to accomplish with this late house: "Here man, intent upon practical improvement, has converted an arid waste into a life-bearing area and, at the same time, has transformed a disconcerting aspect into a pleasing composition."[9]

David Gebhard
University of California
Santa Barbara

7 | Richard J. Neutra, *Wie Baut Amerika?* (Stuttgart: Julius Hoffmann, 1927), 73–77.
8 | Albert Frey, op. cit., 21.
9 | Ibid.

The Early Years, 1903–30

1.1   1.2

A YOUNG BOY, about ten years old, watched his father and uncles construct a small metal shed adjacent to their family business [fig. 1.1]. He was amazed at how fast they assembled it, and this left an indelible impression on the boy that would become the foundation for his ideology as a young architect. Later, this impression would travel with him to America and, in time, he would become one of the innovative thinkers of the American modern movement.[1]

Born on October 18, 1903 in Zurich, Switzerland, Albert Frey was the only son of Ida (1874–1942) and Albert (1870–1947) Frey,[2] an upper-middle-class couple who were well educated in the arts [fig. 1.2, c. 1922]. Frey senior was in partnership with his brothers in a lithography and printing business that their grandfather had started. Frey attributed his desire to become an architect to his father, who had originally wanted to be an architect, but being an eldest son was trained to go into the family business and subsequently to become its creative director. Unable to realize his own desires, Frey's father persuaded his youngest brother, Hugo, to become an architect, but after a few years of designing traditional Swiss houses Hugo abandoned the profession to teach watercolor painting. Frey's mother, Ida, was educated in a music conservatory in Zurich, and after graduating taught music and gave recitals, eventually putting her professional career aside to start a family.[3]

As a child, Frey was surrounded by both the arts and technology. The family lived adjacent to the printing and lithography shop in a mixed-use residential and industrial area of Zurich. Frey's father was an avid painter of still lifes and landscapes, and the family's vast library contained many volumes of classical literature and books on Impressionist artists. On many evenings the family would sit around the dining room table in silence reading the classics, except for Frey, who would be engrossed in books on travel and exploration.[4]

Frey's determination and keen sense of experimentation was evident early in his life. From 1921 to 1923, he built several canoes out of bent-wood frames and canvas, persevering until he was successful in keeping them from turning over in the water. He also constructed a camera for himself, with bellows made from his mother's old gloves.[5]

Frey received his formal architectural education at the Institute of Technology in Winterthur, Switzerland, earning his diploma in 1924. Trained in traditional building construction, he received technical instruction rather than a design education in the then-accepted Beaux Arts tradition.[6] Before he received his diploma he was apprenticed for two years with the architect A. J. Arter in Zurich, and also did construction work during

1 | Joseph Rosa interview with Albert Frey, 27 June 1987.
2 | Rosa interview with Frey, 14 November 1986.
3 | Rosa interview with Frey, 27 June 1987.
4 | Ibid.
5 | Rosa interview with Frey, 28 June 1987.
6 | Rosa interview with Frey, 4 July 1987; Anne van Loo and Dario Matteoni, eds., Sharon Krengel, trans., "Belgian Modernism: Themes and Projects." *Rassegna* (*L'architettura in Belgio 1920–1940 / Architecture in Belgium 1920–1940*), 34, 35.

 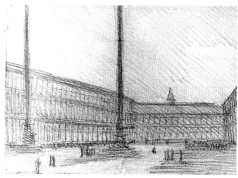

1.3 1.4

his school vacations. It was around this time that Frey began to discover the modern movement from reading periodicals such as the German magazine *Wasmuth* and the Swiss *Werk*, which in 1925 devoted one issue solely to the Brussels modern movement, and from viewing exhibitions at the *Gewerbschule* in Zurich (a trade school established along the lines of the Bauhaus). It was through these sources that Frey first became aware of De Stijl, the Bauhaus, and the modern movement in Brussels. Their new ideas fascinated him and inspired him to think about the possibilities of architecture in the broader scope outside of Switzerland.[7]

Feeling that his education in design had been incomplete, Frey traveled to Italy after graduation. His sketches from this trip show his ability to see the relationship of form to open space, and the effect of light on space. In Venice he found the Piazza San Marco to be a "fantastic outdoor room," and in all of his sketches of it he simplified the details and stripped the buildings down to their bare elements [figs. 1.3, 1.4].[8] The ornate details did not interest him; what were important were the forms and how they were combined to create space.

Frey sensed that his opportunities to design modern architecture in Zurich were limited. Most of the architects building in the new modern style taught at the Technical University in Zurich and hired their own students to work for them. Moreover, Frey had become acquainted with the modern movements in Europe and America and realized there was more to modern architecture than what he had encountered in Switzerland. In September of 1925, he moved to Brussels to pursue his quest to build modern architecture. (At the time, it was not possible for a German Swiss national to get a work permit in France, which would have been the ideal place for him.) He was excited by the possibilities of working in a French-speaking country, and arrived in Brussels with a list of architects for whom he wished to work, first approaching Victor Bourgeois, the leader of the Brussels modern movement. Bourgeois, however, was not hiring and sent Frey to his colleagues Jean-Jules Eggericx and Raphael Verwilghen, who were also prominent in the movement and who hired him immediately.[9]

After World War I, Belgium had a severe housing shortage, which allowed many of the young architects returning to private practice to design buildings in light of the new modern ideas. Eggericx and Verwilghen, both of whom had spent the war in England, returned to Brussels filled with new knowledge in planning and architecture from sources such as Ebenezer Howard's Garden City and Herman Muthesius's writings on the English house.[10] The ideas to which Frey was exposed and the buildings on which he

7 | Ibid.
8 | Rosa interview with Frey, 5 July 1987.
9 | Rosa interview with Frey, 4 July 1987; van Loo and Matteoni, eds., op. cit., 35.
10 | Ibid.

1.5

1.6
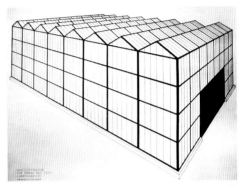
1.7
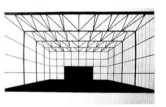
1.8

worked during this period would form the basis for his own ideas about housing when he came to America.

The Floréal and Le Logis housing complexes in Boitsfort near Brussels [fig. 1.5, 1922–30], the first buildings on which Frey worked for Eggericx, are considered to be some of the most significant housing complexes built in Belgium at the time. The designs of these *cités jardins* were generally modeled after those of the Dutch and English garden city movements. The planning was done by the architect and urban planner Louis van der Swaelmen, while Eggericx was one of three architects commissioned to design and supervise the construction of the housing. The Fer à Cheval apartment building [fig. 1.6, 1924–30], the second project on which Frey worked, was constructed on one of the most visible sites in Floréal. It functioned as a commercial center with three stories of apartments above shops and a nine-story residential tower at the center. The massing of the low-rise structure is articulated by a projecting floor slab at each level. In contrast to the horizontal low-rise wings, the verticality of the tower is dramatized by a continuous glass-block window at the stair that rises above the entry doors and passes through the only projecting horizontal slab at the roof plane. Above this projected plane is a brick parapet that is gently curved back against the sky; the tower then becomes a monumental civic structure that serves to conceal the city's water supply tanks. Frey worked primarily on the detailing of these projects, as both were already underway when he arrived in Brussels.[11]

While working in Brussels, Frey discovered the Amsterdam magazine *Wendingen* and Le Corbusier's book *Towards a New Architecture*. He had been acquainted with the work of Le Corbusier, and found the pure Corbusian aesthetic more appealing than the political dogma of many of the other architects in Europe. He came to the realization that he wanted to work only in the modern idiom, and that his beliefs were more sympathetic with Le Corbusier's than with those expressed by the cooperatively designed, socialist housing he was developing in Belgium. He therefore decided that he wanted to work in the atelier of Le Corbusier, and left Eggericx and Verwilghen in February of 1927 to move back to his family in Zurich in order to save money to go on to Paris. Until October of 1928, he worked for Leuenberger, Fluckiger doing detailing and construction drawings of traditional cooperative housing—only a brief detour on his journey to Paris.[12]

By 1927 Frey had already formulated a strong ideology of his own. At Leuenberger, Fluckiger he worked on many personal projects and competitions in an attempt to explore his own ideas. A Factory of Steel and Glass [figs. 1.7, 1.8] and a

11 | Ibid.
12 | Rosa interview with Frey, 15 November 1986, 18 July 1987.

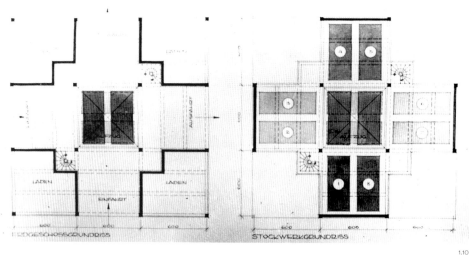
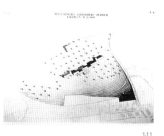

Concrete Parking Tower [figs. 1.9, 1.10] of poured concrete with infill panels, both projects of 1927, primarily expressed structure and function. Both were in keeping with Le Corbusier's lyrical machine aesthetic and minimalist functionalism. The plan of the parking garage is based on a nine-square grid in which the central cruciform shape rises to become a ten-story tower for eighty cars. The four corner squares are one-story commercial structures, while the center of the cruciform houses an exposed elevator. Frey's interpretation of the machine aesthetic, however, differs from Le Corbusier's. The parking garage tower typifies this fundamental difference since the building glorifies the machine by exposing the structure of the elevator and all of its mechanisms, and it is this elevator tower, which is taller than the four concrete parking towers, that becomes the central focus of the building. The building's function as a large machine is overtly emphasized: one drives into the heart of this machine and rises into the air to park a car.

In 1928, Frey entered a competition entitled "Housing for the Old" [figs. 1.11, 1.12] and demonstrated his ability to work in the modern idiom on a large scale. His building is a symmetrical, linear scheme with a single-loaded corridor and horizontal bands of windows. To break up the monotony of its length, Frey articulated the dwelling to recede as one approaches the north side of the building. On this elevation a series of narrow, horizontal bands of windows expresses the corridors that lead to the private rooms, but also gives this side an institutional appearance. The only change in fenestration occurs at the central pavilion, which houses the communal facilities, and from which extends the axis by which one approaches the building by car. The private rooms are at the south side, which is anything but institutional, with large areas of glass open to the light, air, and views. The difference between the two elevations is further expressed in the landscaping. The grounds on the south side have meandering foot paths that move through the natural terrain, in contrast to the axial approach to the central pavilion on the north side, which could only be experienced via automobile.

Frey's preoccupation with housing was evident as early as 1928 with the Minimal Metal House [figs. 1.13, 1.14, project], a house meant to be affordable by the general public. The house is minimal in that all of the private spaces and the kitchen spin off of the living area, eliminating the need for corridors. Each room has built-in cabinets to maximize storage. The exterior wall of the living area is composed of large, glass sliding doors with sliding screened louvers hung from a track on the exterior that could be used to block the sun. This is the first project in which he used corrugated metal as an exterior sheathing material, and it is very reminiscent of the metal shed constructed by his father.

MINIMAL METAL HOUSE, 1928

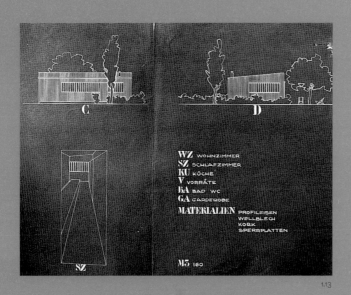

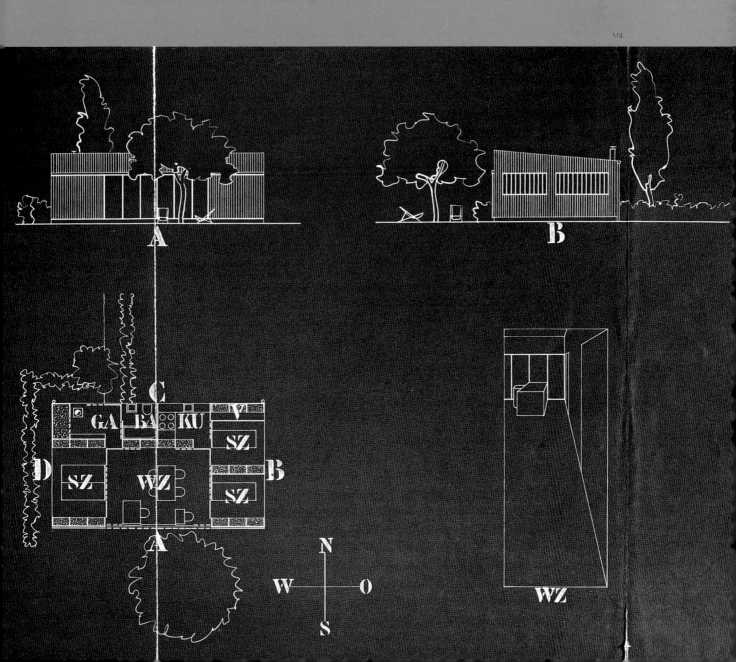

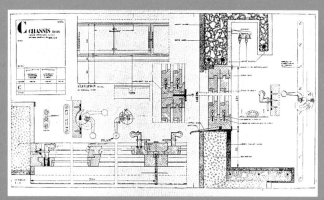

1.15

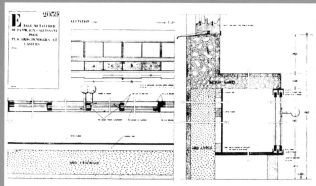

1.16

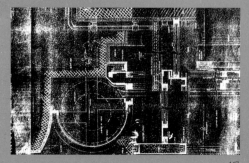

1.17

1.18

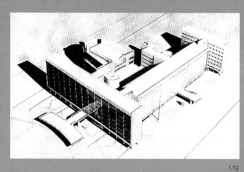

1.19

1.20

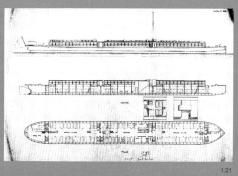

1.21

1.22

The house shows Frey's interpretation of Le Corbusier's ideas, with its extensive use of built-in cabinets and compact spatial arrangements. Later, in the early 1930s, Frey would explore these issues and write about them in America with A. Lawrence Kocher (*see* Selected Bibliography: Writings by Albert Frey, page 146).

Enthusiasm for America and what it represented was sweeping Europe. Everything new and exciting seemed to originate in America, from the technology that resulted in the skyscraper to the jazz that was being played across the continent. For the post-World War I culture in Europe, America was not necessarily the ideal, but it was the only country at the forefront of progress. With the implementation of the ideas of standardization, Taylorization (scientific management), and Fordism in America, the industrial aesthetic was born. These American ideas particularly provoked the interest of European architects. Frey's sense of progressiveness and inventiveness attracted him to what America represented—a country where technology and the spirit of progress were embraced. In the early part of 1928, he applied for a visa to the United States, which, at the time, usually took almost two years to obtain.

Frey's desire to come to America only reinforced his need to work under Le Corbusier first.[13] After saving enough money in Zurich, Frey went to Paris in October of 1928. He was permitted to enter France on a student visa. On his first morning, he set out early to the atelier of Le Corbusier and Pierre Jeanneret. He met with Jeanneret (Le Corbusier always painted at home in the mornings) and showed him his portfolio, which consisted of his personal projects and the work with Eggericx and Verwilghen. Jeanneret told him: "We could use you," and within a week, Frey was working in the atelier full-time. He met with Le Corbusier on his first afternoon when Le Corbusier went on his regular rounds with Jeanneret, stopping at each table to review and critique the progress of the work. Frey and Ernest Weissman were the only full-time, salaried employees at the time. While Frey was there, his peers included José Luis Sert, Kunio Maekawa, and Charlotte Perriand.[14]

The years 1928–29 marked a pivotal point in Le Corbusier's career. He received commissions for the Villa Savoye, Poissy [figs. 1.15–1.18]; Centrosoyus Administration Building, Moscow [fig. 1.19]; Villa Church, Ville d'Avray; Maison Loucheur [fig. 1.20, project], France; *Cité de Refuge* (Salvation Army), Paris; *Asile Flottant*, Paris [figs. 1,21, 1.22]; League of Nations Palace (project II), Geneva; Prager Factory (project), France; and the Mundaneum (project), Geneva. Frey was able to work on all of these projects in the ten months that he was in the atelier, from October 1928 to July 14, 1929.[15]

Le Corbusier worked closely with Frey on his first project at the atelier, the Centrosoyus Administration Building. Frey built the model, rendered over photographs of the model, and did elevation drawings and the axonometric diagram of Le Corbusier's neutralizing wall system.[16] He also worked closely with Jeanneret designing and developing standardized details for the windows and built-in cabinetry used in the Villa Savoye, the Maison Loucheur project, and later residences. One innovative detail they developed together was a mechanism to lock the windows in place; it was made of an S-shaped plate that would tighten the window in position and was attached to a lever with a small ball designed to fit into the palm of the hand.[17] The cabinetry Frey designed consisted of a long horizontal unit with sliding doors of very thin, gauged aluminum, the length of which was determined by the length of a horizontal band of windows above. The handles were made of metal tubing with a small ball attached, resembling the balls on the window locks. Thus, all the mechanisms meant to be moved by hand shared a common form, whether they were used for opening a door, a window, or a cabinet. It should be noted that this built-in cabinetry was similar in detail, but not in

11 | Ibid.
12 | Rosa interview with Frey, 15 November 1986, 18 July 1987.
13 | Ibid; Thomas P. Hughes, *American Genesis* (New York: Viking Penguin, 1989), 249; Marie-Odile Briot, Gladys C. Fabre, and Barbara Rose, *Leger and the Modern Spirit 1918–1931* (Paris: Societe des Amis du Musee d'Art Moderne, 1982), 85.
14 | Rosa interview with Frey, 18 July 1987; Alfred Roth to Joseph Rosa, 14 September 1988; Le Corbusier atelier black log book, Fondation Le Corbusier, Paris.
15 | This listing of projects and buildings is assembled from interviews with Albert Frey and from the black log book that was used in Le Corbusier's atelier to record most of the drawing that was done; this was usually is signed by the draftsman. The log book confirms this listing with the exception of the Cité De Refuge, League of Nations Palace (competition II) and the Mundaneum, all of which are not listed in the book. No record exists in the Fondation Le Corbusier of who worked on these projects.
16 | Rosa interview with Frey, 19 July 1987; black log book no. 2088, FLC.
17 | Ibid; black log books nos. 2036 and 2039, FLC.
18 | Ibid.

design, to the cabinetry designed for the library in the music pavilion of the Villa Church, on which Frey also worked.[18]

One of the most significant contributions Frey made while at the atelier was his work on Villa Savoye. He prepared many of the construction drawings for the house, from the tile chaise in the bathroom to details for the large, glass sliding door that opens onto the terrace from the living room. The door, unusual at the time, was hung from a track on the ceiling—an idea Frey borrowed from a detail in *Sweet's Catalog* for sliding barn-door hardware. The hardware for the door was custom-made in France, although such products were standard in America. Numerous other details were also assimilated from *Sweet's*, which in the early 1920s consisted of only one volume that was about an inch thick.[19]

The Maison Loucheur, a proposal on which Frey worked intermittently, was the only project to which he contributed from the outset, allowing him to work with Le Corbusier on the actual design process. Many schemes were developed. One of the lesser-known involved a freestanding house on pilotis for which Frey did many design studies of a minimal bathroom. Another variation showed the shower and water closet together in one space, sharing a drain.[20] The overall plan of this scheme would later serve as a model for Frey's Ralph-Barbarin House (1932) and his Subsistence Farmsteads (project, 1934).

Probably the most unusual commission Le Corbusier ever received, besides one to design a dog kennel (never executed) adjacent to the gate house of Villa Savoye, was the *Asile Flottant* (1929).[21] He was commissioned by the *Cité de Refuge* to transform a concrete barge into a shelter for the vagrants and prostitutes of Paris. Frey found the boat to be "an interesting problem, entirely different from anything else." He worked on construction drawings, executing plans and sections that showed the connection of the barge to the new structure.[22]

The combination of Le Corbusier's ideology and a shared interest in American technology led to a stimulating and productive work environment for Frey. Part of the reason Frey had wanted to work with Le Corbusier was "that he was building more along the American technique than Frank Lloyd Wright. He did not have the ornamentation that Wright had, which in a way was not American." Frey's vision of America, which he had been cultivating since childhood, came from popular magazines, travel books, Erich Mendelsohn's *Amerika* and Richard Neutra's *Wie Baut Amerika?* American architecture, however, would be more of a new frontier to him than he realized, for he was unfamiliar with the American vernacular.[23]

Le Corbusier knew of Frey's desire to go to America and would jokingly refer to him as "this American guy."[24] In the winter of 1929, Frey received word that his visa to America had been approved. He left the atelier with Le Corbusier's respect and admiration, and the two kept in touch with each other for many years. Frey had barely made enough money to support himself in Paris, however, so he needed to earn more money for the trip. He left Le Corbusier's atelier on July 14, 1929, and after a vacation in a little fishing village near Toulon with his family and Kunio Maekawa, returned to Brussels to work for Eggericx and Verwilghen again, this time as their chief designer.[25]

While at Eggericx and Verwilghen's office, Frey designed an office building from October 1929 to August 1930 that placed second in a competition, and worked on the planning and design for two cities in the Belgian Congo (now Zaire): Uvira and Bukavu [figs. 1.23–1.27, projects], located in the region of Kivu. He worked with Verwilghen on the development of the plans for both of these cities and developed the architectural program for Bukavu.[26]

---

19 | Ibid; black log books nos. 2089, 2122, 2131, 2134, 2136, 2137, 2138, 2141, 2146, 2148, 2152, 2158, 2160, 2162, 2171, and 2172, FLC.

20 | Ibid; black log books nos. 2018, 2051, and 2053, FLC.

21 | Tim Benton, *The Villas of Le Corbusier 1920–1930* (New Haven: Yale University Press, 1987), 205.

22 | Rosa interview with Frey, 27 July 1987; Willy Boesiger, ed., *Le Corbusier et Pierre Jeanneret Oeuvre Complète 1929–1934* (Zurich: Les Editions d'Architeture Artemis, 1964), 32.

23 | Rosa interview with Frey, 27 July 1987.

24 | Ibid.

25 | Ibid.

26 | Rosa interview with Frey, 5 July 1987.

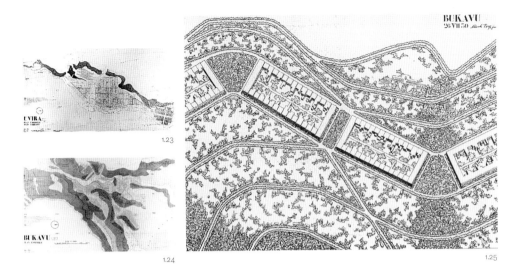

1.23
1.24
1.25

The planning schemes for Uvira [fig. 1.23] and Bukavu [figs. 1.24–1.27] differ from each other due to the typology of the land and its use. Uvira rests on a slightly sloped site between mountains and a lake. An orthogonal grid is imposed on the site, which allowed for the separation of commercial and residential zones as well as the separation of black and white neighborhoods. No buildings were designed for this site. Bukavu, on the other hand, sits on the ridge of a hill. The commercial area is at the top of the ridge with single-family homes terracing down the sides. Both the commercial and residential areas follow the contours of the hill and the whole city is interspersed with parks. The planning concepts were derived from an American magazine on city planning called *The American City*. Although neither plan was ever executed,[27] the experience of working on city planning of this scale would be an asset to Frey in the 1940s when he began to design buildings for the yet-undeveloped resort of Palm Springs, California.

27 | Ibid.

1.26

1.27

THE EARLY YEARS, 1903–30 : 11

letters

New Year's Eve, 1928, at Le Corbusier and Jeanneret's atelier after working late on a charette for Centrosoyus; (L to R) Ernest Weissman, Le Corbusier, N. Kolli, Albert Frey, P. Nahman, Charlotte Perriand, and Pierre Jeanneret.

July 5, 1934
Paris

My dear Frey,
Thank you for your May 20th letter. I have only taken so long to answer it because I have been abroad several times.

It is so kind of you to keep in touch with me so often; it gives me the greatest pleasure to hear from you. I am certain that you will be able to produce some interesting things.

You write to me of the book "CROISADE." It came out in the month of October last year in the Esprit Nouveau series.

If the *PRELUDE* magazines interest you, you should try to circulate them a bit in the United States and get some of your friends to subscribe.

The cost is minimal: 15 French francs per year.

Its ideas must be spread amongst milieus such as yours.

Do not forget that I would still be interested in coming to the United States once, invited by whomever, to give a series of lectures on urban planning. I have come to various conclusions for the city as well as for the countryside, which might interest professionals and the public opinion there.

Give my regards to Raymond [sic] Kocher.

Sincerely,

26 October 1934
Paris

My dear Frey,
You are a good man, you keep in touch, which always gives me great pleasure. You now write French like an "Academy man!" What is good about you is that you are very lively, that you see things as a whole and with personal vision, personal judgement and personal reactions.

You make me envious when speaking to me about coming to America. I would be extremely interested. I will say, as you do by the way, and do not take this statement as vanity: "I really have things to say in America, because my conclusions, after so many years of work, are of a nature that they should be an integral part of all national reorganization programs. The world has become sickened from a guilty conscience, and this conscience directly ties itself to the conditions of life, and life is but an activity that occurs at the heart of the house, the city and the country."

If you can help to organize my trip to America, I would gratefully accept. But as the dollar isn't worth much anymore, I will require much more than what was offered to me the other times. Please understand: as I keep playing Peter the Hermit I end up broke and that becomes disagreeable at a certain age.

Give Kocher my regards.

Your friend,

P.S. Your house photos are very beautiful. Believe it or not, I had a few years ago, while staying at the seaside, accepted the principle of making wood houses covered with canvas and waterproofed, as boats are, with special paint. But my houses were formed from members 2.75 meters wide by a depth to be determined, and these members were added one next to the other for the enlargement of the house. But the principle of wood and canvas was the same, with different architectural results, of course. What I like about your little house is that it is quite clear, and mostly that it is built; that is a great virtue.

November 10, 1935
Palm Springs, California

Dear Mr. Le Corbusier,
It was with tremendous joy that I learned of your arrival in New York. Mr. Kocher is keeping me up to date. He wrote to me that the length of your stay in the United States was limited and that you would have to return to France before having the possibility of taking a trip Out West. This is really too bad, "New York is not America," Americans say. The east coast of the U.S. is still quite European, enlarged to grotesque proportions; it is in the new towns Out West, established during the evolution of the automobile, where modern American life is found. In Los Angeles, commercial buildings are clustered at the intersections of main thoroughfares; the town is spread out, not concentrated, it's true, but one travels at 40 km and traffic keeps moving

Temporarily, I have the opportunity to practice in the exclusive location of Palm Springs, which extends into the desert, at the foot of a mountain range not far from Los Angeles. A winter resort *par excellance* [sic] for the elite in business, industry and the intellect, it provides the rare pleasure of combining a magnificent natural environment with being a center for interesting and varied activities. Moreover, the sun, the pure air and the simple forms of the desert create perfect conditions for architecture.

I had privately hoped to see you on American soil and it is regrettable that it is not possible at this time. But judging from the definite progress that modern architecture is now making in the United States, I feel that there will one day be a great project here for you. So I say good bye my dear Le Corbusier.

Yours,

Albert Frey

April 22, 1936
Palm Springs, California

Dear Mr. Le Corbusier,

The California desert continues to charm me, continues to nourish me, to give me an opportunity for modern architecture, from time to time. It is a most interesting experience to live in a wild, savage, natural setting, far from the big city, but without losing contact with civilization, thanks to the car (120 miles to Los Angeles, or 2 hours), to the radio, to the plane and to the intellectual milieu in Palm Springs due to the presence of visitors and inhabitants from all parts of the world. I am working with a young American who manages the [Palm Springs] offices of Van Pelt & Lind Architects. I am enclosing the issue of *Arch. Record* which contains several pages on our work. I was in charge of the design, the construction and the furnishing of the Guthrie House. We are confident that the future holds more and more opportunities to do modern work. Our hopes are based on the fact that traditional architecture here is an imitation of simple Mexican houses which are often quite modern in terms of the composition of space.

Fortunately our efforts are not hindered by building codes regulating size, style or materials. The result of this freedom is that parcels of land look like laboratories of architectural and materials research.

In fact, all American cities look this way, as I'm sure you noticed. Fortunately, also, one only expects a house to last 30 years. They are consequently not built to last. As I have settled in America I had to understand and accept the psychology of life here so not to be in constant conflict, and also in order to earn a living. I play upon the fact that for the American, progress is achieved more by practical experimentation than by mental query; new habits and new forms are equally accepted through gradual usage or exposure. Only mechanical, scientific, and technical progress is accepted without hesitation; they blindly believe in the infallibility of the engineer and the technician.

Currently I am studying your book entitled *La Ville Radieuse*. Its contents give me the courage sometimes needed to fight against the reactionaries. Your eloquence is undeniable and I admire your perseverance; the book is the testament of modern architecture, it analyzes all the problems, it proposes all the solutions, it is a masterpiece. It should bring encouragement and happiness to many young and aspiring architects.

I wish you the greatest success for the realization of magnificent projects. Are you going to have an exhibit at the next exposition in Paris? My regards to you and Mr. Jeanneret.

Sincerely yours.

Albert Frey

21 January 1937
Paris

My dear Frey,
I am answering, quite late, your letter dated April 22. I was in Brazil in the interim and to Rome after that and went on additional trips. You will, therefore, please excuse me.

Your letters are always of great interest and I congratulate you on your creations, which are always very pure and original. I believe you are really on the right track and I enjoy seeing your works.

Thank you for your appraisal of *La Ville Radieuse*. It is, in effect, quite a large undertaking that was done, not at all for personal gain, since in reality, there is but work done on paper. Will something come of it one day? We don't know. It is the unknown, but I believe that when one firmly knows a truth, it is one's duty to express it. It is this, by the way, that I like about you; it is that you do not make compromises.

The publisher *PLON* has put on the market just yesterday my new book on America, *When the Cathedrals Were White*. The terms of the publishing are such that it is impossible to send copies to one's friends, for which I apologize. I was able, on the other hand, to send one to Lawrence Kocher, as he is a magazine director. If you read my book, I would be curious to know your opinion of it.

With fond remembrance and wishing you courage.

America, the East Coast, 1930–39

FREY ARRIVED IN New York on September 5, 1930, and shortly thereafter began working with A. Lawrence Kocher (1885–1969) in a partnership that would last until March 1935, with another brief collaboration in 1938. Kocher's previous associate, Gerhard Ziegler, had recently returned to Europe.[1] At the time, Kocher was the managing editor of *Architectural Record*. He was already established as a modern architect with his Sunlight Towers (project, 1929) and the Rex Stout House (1929) in Fairfield County, Connecticut—the first poured concrete house on the East Coast. Although trained in the Beaux Arts tradition, Kocher was a true Renaissance man; with an art and art history background, he then studied architecture at the Massachusetts Institute of Technology. He joined the staff of *Architectural Record* in 1928 and turned it into a forum for modern architecture.[2]

Since their office consisted solely of Frey and Kocher, Frey worked on the projects at the office during the day while Kocher was at *Architectural Record*. In the evening, they would discuss the progress of the work. It was commonly known that "Frey was the designer and Kocher was the writer and the front man...Frey was an artist."[3] Kocher and Frey were a perfect team; each possessed what the other may have lacked. Frey did not have to concern himself with specifications, clients (of which there were few), or promoting their work. He was left to design, with Kocher playing the role of critic. Throughout his career, Frey's partners would fill a similar role, allowing him to remain private and out of the public eye.

Although Kocher and Frey only built four buildings during the course of their partnership, their contribution to the American modern movement was significant. They coauthored many articles on urban planning, the modern aesthetic, and technology for *Architectural Record*, which established theirs as one of the most innovative and influential partnerships in America during the early 1930s. Exploring the latest in American building technology, their projects for low-cost, experimental, and prefabricated housing were published internationally, placing them at the forefront of the American modern movement.

When modernist European architects came to the United States as early as 1914, they usually began by working on the East Coast, and then sometimes moved on to build their careers on the West Coast, as did R. M. Schindler, Richard Neutra, J. R. Davidson, and Kem Weber. With the exception of William Lescaze and Frederick Kiesler, who stayed in New York and built their first structures there (Lescaze's Capital Bus Terminal, 1927, and Kiesler's Film Guild Cinema, 1929), this remained the usual model until the late 1920s. By 1931 the East Coast had an impressive assembly of European and American architects who were educated and trained by the masters in Europe and were

1 | Rosa interview with Frey, 14 November 1986.

2 | The A. Lawrence Kocher Papers, Special Collection, The Colonial Williamsburg Foundation Library.

3 | Rosa interview with Philip Johnson, 28 May 1987.

ALUMINAIRE HOUSE, 1930–31

2.1

2.2

2.3

2.4

2.5

building in New York, Ohio, and Pennsylvania. William Muschenheim, an American who studied under Peter Behrens at the Academy of Fine Arts in Vienna, built the Bath Houses in Hampton Bays, New York, in 1930.[4] Kocher and Frey built the Aluminaire House in 1931. Alfred Clauss, a disciple of Mies van der Rohe,[5] and George Daub designed the prototype for the Standard Oil Gas Stations in 1931, which were constructed across America.

The European ideal of factory-produced prefabricated housing was a reality in America by the mid-1930s. By 1933, numerous prefabricated houses manufactured by American Houses, Inc. and General Houses, Inc. had been built in New York, Connecticut, and Massachusetts.[6] Modernist buildings had at this time, however, become far more prevalent on the West Coast than on the East Coast, where the trend was frequently toward more experimental and theoretical buildings.

Having worked for Le Corbusier and studied his writings, it was natural that Frey would bring his modern technological aesthetic to America—an aesthetic based on a belief in modern architecture as a way of life and not merely a style. Since Frey came to America at a time when social values and ideologies were in a state of transition,[7] the perfect climate was provided in which Frey could experiment with design and expand his theories. Advances were being made in American technology that enabled him to take the ideas of the European modern movement and build on them through the use of new materials. He became thoroughly versed in many of these materials: their properties, limitations, and uses. This is exemplified by his experimentation with metal as an exterior sheathing material, and is believed to have influenced Neutra and others.[8] One fundamental difference between Neutra and Frey is that Neutra would paint wood window frames to simulate a machined metal frame; Frey, on the other hand, would paint both wood and machined frame with color because the window represented a point where light passed through a wall. His buildings are simple, honest expressions of function and materiality.

In September 1930, Kocher was asked by the curator of the annual Allied Arts and Building Products Exhibition to design a project that would attract the general public to their 1931 exhibition, which was to be held jointly with the annual Architectural League Exhibition.[9] Kocher and Frey proposed a full-scale house, which they called the Aluminaire—"A House For Contemporary Life" [figs. 2.1–2.4]. A model was made of it, and suppliers such as the Aluminum Company of America, the McClintic-Marshall Corporation (subsidiary of Bethlehem Steel), and Westinghouse were solicited to donate the materials needed to construct it. Erected in less than ten days, the Aluminaire was the only full-scale house on display at the exhibition [fig. 2.5], which took place at the

4 | Alastair Gordon, *Long Island Modern* (New York: Guild Hall of East Hampton, 1987), 11.

5 | Rosa interview with Alfred Clauss, 19 May 1987.

6 | John McAndrew, ed., *Guide to Modern Architecture* (New York: Museum of Modern Art, 1940), 22, 25, 33, 52, 56; Gilbert Herbert, *The Dream of the Factory-made House: Walter Gropius and Konrad Wachsmann* (Cambridge MA: The MIT Press, 1984), 226–27.

7 | Warren I. Susman, *Culture as History* (New York: Pantheon Books, 1973), 243.

8 | Esther McCoy to Rosa, 2 December 1987.

9 | Rosa interview with Frey, 14 November 1986.

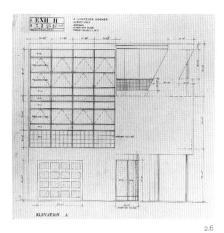
2.6

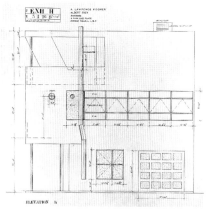
2.7

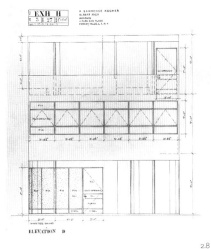
2.8

10 | The A. Lawrence Kocher Papers.

11 | "Aluminaire: A House for a Contemporary Life," *Shelter* 2 (May 1932): 56–58.

12 | Rosa interview with Frey, 25 July 1987.

13 | Hamilton Beatty and Norman N. Rice, both Americans, worked for Le Corbusier and Jeanneret. Rice started in the fall of 1929, Beatty in the fall of 1930, and both were back in the United States by 1931. Rice worked for George Howe & William Lescaze on the PSFS Building in Philadelphia and wrote articles for *Architectual Forum* and *Shelter* magazines, but did not build his own work until the late 1930s. Hamilton Beatty built his first structure, a house, in the late summer of 1931 in Madison, Wisconsin, in collaboration with his wife Gwendydd. Rosa interview with Bill Strauss (nephew and holder of Norman N. Rice Papers), 16 May 1989; interview with Hamilton Beatty, 22 May 1989; black log book, FLC.

14 | F. R. S. Yorke, *The Modern House* (London: The Architectural Press, 1934), 181, 182.

15 | Ibid.

Grand Central Palace in New York from April 18 through 25, 1931.[10] Its actual size was dictated by the size of the exhibition space.[11] The Aluminaire was the first building designed by a disciple of Le Corbusier[12]—and the first all-light-steel-and-aluminum house—to be constructed in America.[13] Aesthetically, it is a neoplastic object, a pure form devoid of vernacular reference and metaphor, designed independently of a site [figs. 2.6–2.9]. It is an assembly of standard, machined materials, but it does not itself evoke the metaphor of the machine, much like Le Corbusier's Citrohan project of 1921.

The house was designed to demonstrate the possibilities of affordable housing achieved through modern technology (it would have cost only $3,200 if it had been mass-produced in quantities of ten thousand or more).[14] Its two elevated levels are supported by six five-inch-diameter aluminum columns attached to aluminum-and-steel channel girders. These support lightweight steel beams covered with a battle-deck—pressed-steel flooring layered with linoleum on insulation board. The walls are nonbearing and act merely as screens. On the exterior walls, narrow-ribbed aluminum is backed with insulation board covered with building paper. This assembly is joined by aluminum washers and screws. The walls are only three inches thick, but were promoted as having a higher insulation value than a thirteen-inch-thick masonry wall. All of the window sashes, doors, and frames are steel.[15]

Most of the furniture is built-in, including a retractable dining table [figs. 2.10–2.12]. Unfortunately, some of the freestanding furniture designed for the house was not built, including a glass card table (which was later built for Kocher's Canvas Weekend House, 1934), an extendable spiral stool [fig. 2.13], and a chair [fig. 2.14] and chaise constructed of rubber, which could be inflated with an air hose and deflated for storage. These inflatable pieces were similar to Le Corbusier and Perriand's designs of the late 1920s; the chaise form resembled the tiled version in the Villa Savoye's master bathroom.

FLOOR 1

FLOOR 2

FLOOR 3

2.9

ALUMINAIRE HOUSE, 1930–31

2.10

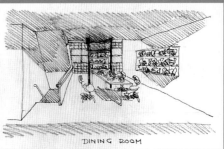

2.11

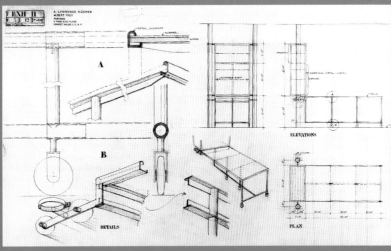

2.12

2.13

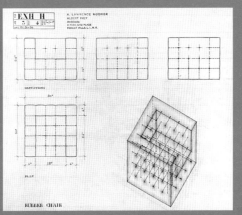

2.14

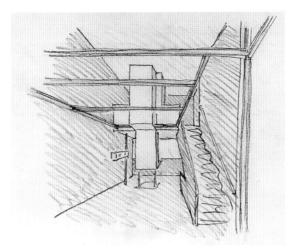
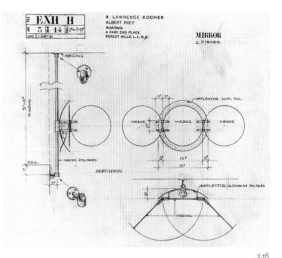

2.15

2.16

At the ground level are a drive-through garage, an open-air porch, an entry, a dumbwaiter, and utilities. The floor above is the only one that encompasses the whole area of the volume. Here, the bedroom, which was to have beds suspended from the ceiling, is separated from an exercise room and bathroom by a folding screen. The living room is a seventeen-foot-high, two-story space [fig. 2.15], separated from the dining room by a built-in glass-and-metal-framed china cupboard that houses an extendable dining room table. The table's rubber top retracts around a cylinder, somewhat like a window shade. On opposite sides of the cupboard are two pipes that service the bathroom above, the shower stall of which cantilevers into the living room. The house was designed to be independent of daylight. In the living room, for instance, multicolored neon lights with reflectors were recessed into the ceiling above the window and in front of the window frame at the second floor level. One was an ultraviolet light for tanning and the other could be used to simulate daylight in the evening [fig. 2.16]. The top floor contains a library, the bathroom with the cantilevered shower stall, and a roof terrace floored in resilient asphalt tile with a parapet sheathed on the inside in asbestos-cement board [figs. 2.17, 2.18].[16]

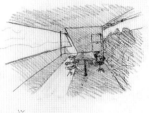

above: 2.17; opposite: 2.18

The Aluminaire House quickly became the central attraction at the Allied Arts and Architectural League Exhibition (which was open for only one week and was attended by 100,000 visitors) and it received a vast amount of press coverage. Because of the speed with which the Aluminaire was erected, the newspapers and popular journals referred to it as the Zipper House and Magic House; they also declared it a viable new model for domestic modern living. The *Time* magazine review of the exhibition referred to the Magic House as "a complete three-story affair of polished aluminum and glass, designed to take the place of the rows of jerry-built Olde Englysshe cottages for families of modest means which speckle U. S. suburbs.... [T]he Magic House has no excavated basement. The owner enters through the garage, climbs a staircase near the oil burning furnace room to a duplex living room, [and] dining room."[17] Deems Taylor's review in "Word and Music" for the *Brooklyn Eagle* also expresses the public's excitement upon experiencing the Aluminaire House: "I saw the 'zipper' house at the architectural show. Its real name is Aluminaire, but having learned that one of its virtues is speed of erection and demolition, promptly decided that the former name was more appropriate. So 'zipper' it was, all last week, to the crowds who never wearied of climbing its stairways, poking through its rooms, and hanging around to discuss it."[18]

16 | Rosa interview with Frey, 25 July 1987.
17 | "Two Years, Architecture," *Time*, 17 April 1931.
18 | Deems Taylor, "Words and Music," *Brooklyn Eagle*, 18 April, 1931.

ALUMINAIRE HOUSE UNDER RECONSTRUCTION

2.19

2.20

2.21   2.22

The criticism the Aluminaire received in the press was mostly due to the effects that this austere modern idiom might have on family life. In Elsie McCormick's review "A Piece of Her Mind," for the *New York World-Telegram*, she imagined the modern interior as a cause of future domestic problems: "It is interesting to speculate on the result of the severely utilitarian lines found in the house of the future. No doubt the stern, office-like effect will produce an atmosphere of great simplicity and unpretentiousness.... There is a danger, however, in making a home look too much like an office. A business man would thus find little relief from his daily surroundings, and it is quite probable that he would be driven to seek escape in fluffier apartments."[19] Hi Philips's review entitled "The Sun Dial—The All Metal Home," for the *New York Sun*, criticized the use of metal in the home: "Now for the 'canned house'! The latest thing in architecture.... When a man resides in one of these things he is practically living in a metal container. If father wants a new door cut through to his room he doesn't get a saw. He gets a can opener."[20] At the close of the exhibition it was made public that the architect Wallace K. Harrison had purchased the house and intended to reconstruct it as a weekend house on his property in Syosset, Long Island.

Harrison bought the house for approximately $1,000,[21] and on April 26th it was disassembled in six hours, and re-erected that May [figs. 2.19, 2.20] on a knoll in Harrison's eleven-acre estate.[22] Reassembling the house took more than ten days and cost substantially more than had been anticipated, in part because the components of the house were left outdoors and a strong rain washed away the identifying chalk numbers, leaving a jigsaw puzzle to be put back together. When it was finally reconstructed, its structural rigidity had been compromised,[23] but photographs of it in this phase frequently have been reprinted in magazines and books illustrating modern architecture in America.

Shortly after Harrison purchased the house, he added two one-story wings to each side of it [fig. 2.21], totally surrounding and subsuming it. These additions had no relationship to the house; eventually, in the early 1940s, the Aluminaire was again relocated and Harrison designed an infill addition between the earlier wings.[24] Used as a guest house on its new site, the Aluminaire was partially buried into a hillside [fig. 2.22], which turned the first floor into a basement. The entrance was relocated to the second floor, which now opened on ground level, and the exterior roof deck was enclosed. The Aluminaire, which once sat elegantly against the horizon, was now reduced to a "tin house," as Harrison called it,[25] placed against the side of a hill and left to deteriorate for the next forty-five years.

Over the years, the Harrison estate changed hands twice. In 1986, the owner applied for a permit to demolish the Aluminaire and divide the land into four parcels for

19 | Elsie McCormick, "A Piece of Her Mind," *New York World-Telegram*, 21 April 1931.
20 | Hi Philips, "The Sun Dial—The All Metal Home," *New York Sun*, 23 April 1931.
21 | Victoria Newhouse, *Wallace K. Harrison, Architect* (New York: Rizzoli International, 1989), 60.
22 | The A. Lawrence Kocher Papers.
23 | Mrs. Wallace K. Harrison to Rosa, 20 May 1987.
24 | Newhouse, op. cit., 63.
25 | Ibid., 60.

26 | I discovered the pending demolition in the course of doing research for the first edition of this book. I went to the local newspapers the *Long Islander, Newsday Long Island,* the *East Hampton Star,* and Paul Goldberger at the *New York Times.* I also solicited architects by telephone and wrote a short essay on the pending status of the Aluminaire House for *Progressive Architecture* (January 1987) to prevent the demolition, and suggested that the Aluminaire could be relocated if an individual or institution would be interested in moving it. This resulted in numerous newspaper articles on the importance of the house and letters of support by prominent architects in the United States and abroad such as Richard Rogers, Peter D. Eisenman, Tod Williams, and John Hedjuk. These efforts made the Huntington Township realize the significance of the Aluminaire, and brought the house to the attention of Jon Michael Schwarting at the New York Institute of Technology. The extensive documentation of the condition in which the house was found, the dismantling and relocation/reconstruction of the Aluminaire on its new site at the School's campus on Carlton Avenue, and fundraising were all supervised by codirectors Jon Michael Schwarting and Frances Campani at the School of Architecture.

27 | Restoration grant from the New York State Department of Parks Recreation and Historic Preservation for $131,750.00.

28 | Rosa interview with Michael Lynch, Restoration Coordinator of Grants for New York State Department of Parks Recreation and Historic Preservation, 26 May 1989; Rosa interview with Jon Michael Schwarting of the New York Institute of Technology, School of Architecture, 8 June 1989.

29 | Terence Riley, *International Style: Exhibition 15 and the Museum of Modern Art* (New York: Rizzoli and Columbia Books of Architecture, 1992), 222; Richard Guy Wilson, Dianne H. Pilgrim, and Dickran Tashjian, *The Machine Age* (New York: Brooklyn Museum and Abrams, 1986), 170.

sale (zoning prohibited two houses on one lot, and the Aluminaire and Harrison houses shared the same land). The permit for demolition was pending approval by the Huntington Township. Enormous efforts were made by the Huntington Historical Society, and by myself and others, to prevent this and to bring the issue to the attention of the public.[26] The house was already listed in the National Register of Historic Places as part of the Harrison estate, but it needed an individual listing with the Huntington local Register of Historic Places to be securely protected. After numerous articles appeared in magazines and newspapers, and many telephone calls soliciting support had been made, the New York Institute of Technology expressed an interest in moving the Aluminaire to the campus of its school of architecture in Central Islip on Long Island. In the fall of 1987, the school was successful in obtaining a restoration grant to cover part of the cost of relocation.[27] The owner then agreed to donate the house to the school. In order to allow the school to move the Aluminaire, it was temporarily removed from the National Register of Historic Places; once it has been fully reconstructed and restored, it will be reevaluated and reinstated to the Register. This time it will be listed in its own right, independent of the site, which will be one of the first such listings for a modern house on the National Register—and appropriate for the Aluminaire, which as a prefabricated house theoretically retains its integrity no matter where it is located.

The preservation of the Aluminaire highlights the contradictions of acquiring historical protection for modernist buildings. Since the modern movement eschewed historical reference, and ideally, traditional construction techniques, progressive architects attracted to new technology tended to work in the modern idiom. But as the period takes its place in time, it also becomes historical. Now, the New York Institute of Technology uses the house to teach students about early attempts at affordable housing, and it stands as an icon of what early modern architecture represented.[28]

Extensively publicized, the Aluminaire was one of the few buildings representing the American modern movement at the acclaimed *International Exhibition of Modern Architecture* curated by Henry-Russell Hitchcock and Philip Johnson at the Museum of Modern Art in 1932. The exhibition; the catalog, entitled *Modern Architecture*; and the book, *The International Style: Architecture Since 1922*, highlighted early modern buildings from all over the world. There were only six buildings from the United States, and two of those were houses: the Aluminaire and Neutra's Lovell House of 1927–29 in California. The exhibition traveled for two years to fourteen locations throughout the United States and played a large role in the development of the American modern movement.[29] Its influence was seen mainly, however, in the development of modern architecture as an applied style in America, in the popularity of the streamline designs that proliferated from the mid-1930s through the late 1940s. Only three American firms were then considered to be truly practicing within the International Style idiom: Kocher and Frey, William Lescaze, and Richard Neutra.[30] Frey, however, would never identify his work with the International Style, feeling that the word "style" implied a period and not a new vision of architecture.[31]

The same month that the Allied Arts and Architectural League Exhibition opened, *Architectural Record* published an article by Kocher & Frey entitled "Real Estate Subdivisions For Low-Cost Housing" [figs. 2.23–2.28]. This proposal presented two

30 | David Gebhard and Harriette Von Breton, *Kem Weber—The Moderne in Southern California 1920 through 1940* (Santa Barbara: University of California, Santa Barbara, 1969), 33.

31 | Rosa interview with Frey, 15 November 1986.

32 | A. Lawrence Kocher and Albert Frey, "Real Estate Subdivisions for Low-Cost Housing," *Architectural Record*, April 1931, 326.

33 | Ibid., 325.

REAL ESTATE SUBDIVISIONS FOR LOW-COST HOUSING, 1930–31

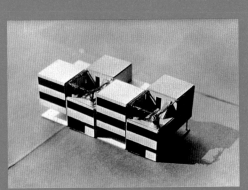

2.23

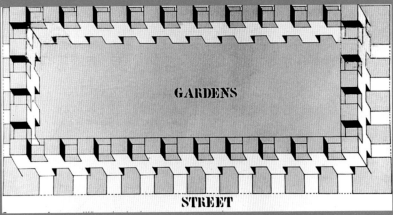

2.24

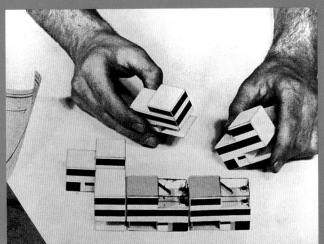

2.25

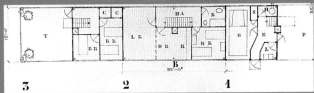

2.26

Continuous Houses (Scheme 1): "Where land values are excessive and recreation areas are nearby it is logical to accept the continuous arrangement. Open porches on the ground floor penetrate the row and establish a relation between street and garden. Free passage of air is admitted to the garden court. Each house is provided with a roof terrace overlooking the garden."[32]

Improved Subdivision (Scheme 2): "Houses are wide and shallow. Broad garden area is at side of house (black indicates blank walls). There is attractiveness and individuality in grouping. There is unobstructed sunlight and privacy because of wide spacing and staggered arrangement. The garage is included in the cube of the house. One driveway services four houses with minimum encroachment on the garden area."[33]

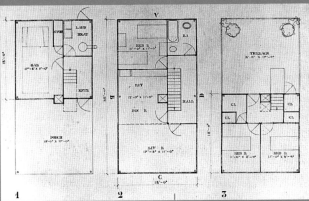

2.27

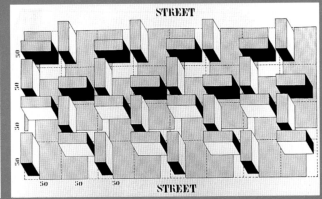

2.28

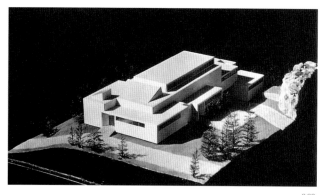

2.29

2.30

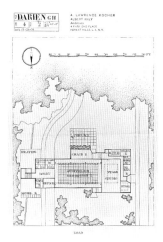

2.31

schemes for improving the shape and use of minimally sized lots for single-family, low-cost housing. The authors expounded the use of a prototypical house, identical to the Aluminaire, and used a principle similar in plan to Le Corbusier's Pessac housing (1925). The entry level of the house is designed to be flexible, in response to the possibility of its use on different sites. In one of their schemes the houses are staggered, allowing for large garden areas between each house, privacy, unobstructed sunlight, and the use of one driveway to serve every four houses. Although never realized, these designs demonstrated the true potential of the Aluminaire as a prototype for housing.[34]

Models and drawings of the Darien Guild Hall [figs. 2.29–2.31, project, 1930], designed at the same time as the Aluminaire, were also shown at the exhibition of 1931, at the Architectural League's separate space. The Guild Hall was to be a community art center for Darien, Connecticut. The volume of each room was developed independently, according to its functional requirements. Once this was done, the elements were placed in functional relationships to each other on the site. The project, unfortunately, was not built, due to a shortage of funds. The commission was predicated on the use of modern industrial materials, which would have cost less than traditional ones, although the proposal did not question traditional construction methods or explore new means of technology.[35] Instead, the building explored functional elements and their interactions with an actual site.

With the final cost of the Aluminaire having been greater than expected, Kocher and Frey looked for alternatives. Since the house had been constructed of components that were not commercially available, they turned their attention to building more inexpensive housing with available materials. They fully explored this problem through two prefabricated farmhouses, called "A" and "B" [figs. 2.32–2.35, project, November 1931], commissioned by the Committee on Farmhouse Design of the President's Conference on Home Building and Home Ownership, of which Kocher was a member.[36] These were designed to include both living and working areas; the information for the architectural program was supplied by sociologists specializing in farm activity. Farmhouse "A" was designed for the Midwest and Farmhouse "B" for the temperate zone. Both were to be constructed from shop-fabricated parts that were readily available in the marketplace and would require only assembly at the site, which would reduce the construction time to seven days for Farmhouse "A" and to four days for Farmhouse "B." This also made the houses more affordable than the Aluminaire: Farmhouse "A" would have cost $3,000 and "B" would have cost $1,500. If produced in quantity, these houses would have been even less expensive.

34 | A. Lawrence Kocher and Albert Frey, "Real Estate Subdivisions for Low-Cost Housing," *Architectural Record*, April 1931, 323–27.

35 | Rosa interview with Frey, 26 July 1987.

36 | Ibid.; The A. Lawrence Kocher Papers.

FARMHOUSE "A," 1931

2.32

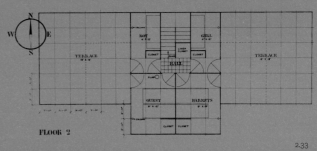

2.33

FARMHOUSE "B," 1931

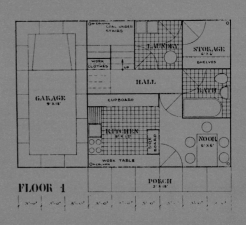

2.34

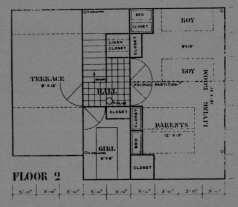

2.35

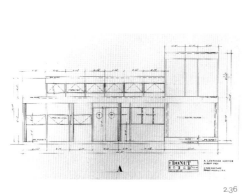

2.36

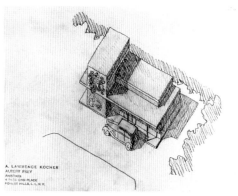

2.37

The structures consisted of light-steel framing with a steel deck floor and roof. Walls were of standard-size panels of 3' x 8' x 1" insulation board clad in metal. The structural module of the buildings allowed for easy replacement of panels and future enlargements, but their life span was expected to be only one generation, with demolition taking twelve hours.[37] With Farmhouse "B," the smaller of the two, Frey started to explore the concept of one multifunctional main space. Here, the living room, where beds are stored against the wall during the day, is converted into two bedrooms by using a folding partition to divide the room.

The farmhouses, however, were not Frey's first proposals for that type of construction. The Downyflake Donut Shop [figs. 2.36–2.38, project], designed five months earlier, used the same system. It was developed through working drawings but was not constructed because the owner was unable to finance it. One feature of the donut shop was a large plate-glass window facing the street where people could watch the donuts being made.[38] All of these projects are similar in concept to Walter Gropius's prefabricated experimental house in the *Weisenhofsiedlung* (1927) in Stuttgart, which Frey had visited in 1927.

37 | Ibid.
38 | Ibid.

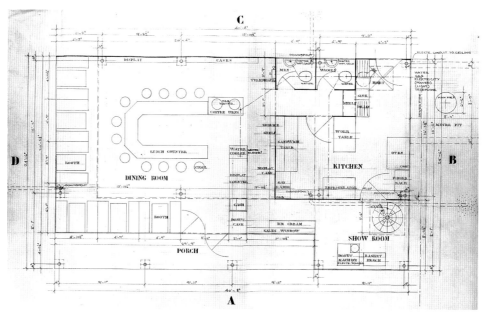

2.38

34 : ALBERT FREY, ARCHITECT

2.39   2.40   2.41

Despite the press that Kocher and Frey had received with the Aluminaire and Kocher's connections through *Architectural Record*, their volume of work was so sparse that from July 1931 to July 1932, Frey worked part-time as a designer for William Lescaze. His designs for Lescaze included the Chrystie-Forsyth Street Housing Development [fig. 2.39, project, 1931–33], the early planning of the River Gardens Housing Project [project, 1931–32], and the Museum of Modern Art [figs. 2.40, 2.41, project, schemes 5 & 6, 1931]. Although none of Frey's work for Lescaze was built, his design for the Chrystie-Forsyth Street Housing Development did establish Lescaze as an architect committed to housing design. The project was for a large-scale, low-cost housing complex that was to cover seven city blocks on the Lower East Side of Manhattan and included twenty-four buildings, each nine stories high with a playground on the roof.[39]

In 1932, Kocher and Frey built their second house, the Ralph-Barbarin House near Stamford, Connecticut. Mrs. Barbarin, one of the two women who commissioned the house, was a retired academic who was knowledgeable about modern architecture and influenced by Le Corbusier's *Towards a New Architecture*.[40] She had read about the Aluminaire and hired Frey and Kocher to design a house adhering to that same ideology.

Two schemes were created. The first was designed to use commercially available materials, like Farmhouses "A" and "B," but was based on design principles similar to the Aluminaire's. In plan, the first floor contained the utilities, garage, and entry; the second floor had an apartment for the owners; and the third floor had a rental apartment. The layout of the second floor was symmetrical, with a vertical circulation spine [figs. 2.42, 2.43]. This plan was very similar to one of the schemes for Le Corbusier's Maison Loucheur. Scheme two, the built version [figs. 2.44, 2.45], has the same massing as the first scheme, but to save money, standard wood-and-masonry construction was used instead of light steel and aluminum. Local contractors were not familiar with steel construction and other modern methods, and consequently the price for using nontraditional construction would have doubled the budget. Double-hung, wood-framed windows were ganged to achieved the effect of a horizontal band of windows.[41] The house tries, in a simple way, to reflect the ideology of the Aluminaire, but does not achieve this due to the budget restrictions. It more resembles its predecessor, the Darien Guild Hall, as an assembly of different functional elements stacked horizontally and tied together by one vertical element, the stair. The first, unbuilt scheme for the Ralph-Barbarin House would have been a finer building, and also a better example of the evolution of Frey's ideas.

39 | Rosa interviews with Frey, 16 November 1986; 22 August 1987; Robert A. M. Stern, *George Howe: Toward a Modern American Architecture* (New Haven: Yale University Press, 1975), 102–37; Richard Pommer, "The Architecture of Urban Housing in the United States During the Early 1930s," *Journal of the Society of Architectural Historians* 37 (December 1978): 251–52; Christian Hubert and Lindsay Stamm Shapiro, *William Lescaze* (New York: Institute for Architecture and Urban Studies/Rizzoli, 1982), 5, 76.
40 | Frey to Le Corbusier, 1936, Fondation Le Corbusier.
41 | Rosa interview with Frey, 26 July 1987.

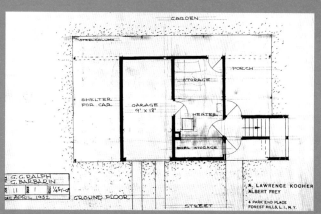
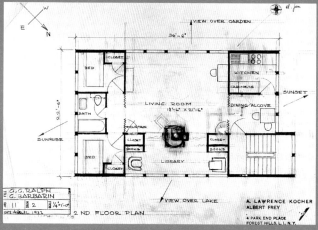
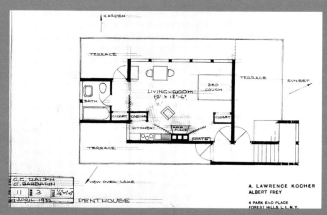

RALPH-BARBARIN HOUSE, SCHEME 1, 1932

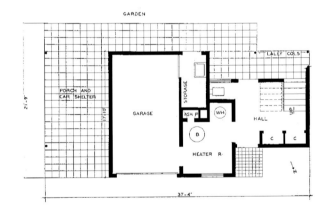

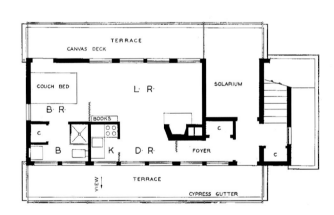

RALPH-BARBARIN HOUSE, SCHEME 2, 1932

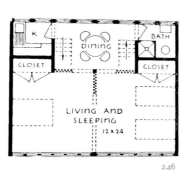

2.46

2.47

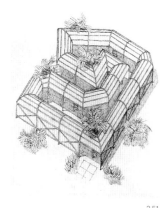

2.51

Commercial industry supplied the impetus for the Experimental Week-end House [figs. 2.46, 2.47, project] and Experimental Five Room House [figs. 2.48–2.50, project]. The Cotton-Textile Institute approached Kocher at *Architectural Record* to see if the use of cotton could be explored in new building technology. Kocher and Frey investigated the idea, which resulted in the design of two houses using cotton canvas as an interior and exterior sheathing material over wood-frame construction.[42] The Experimental Five Room House was raised off the ground plane and supported by eight steel columns. The Experimental Week-end House was supported by four steel columns. A typical wall assembly consisted of 2-x-4 wood studs with insulation board on either side, covered by fireproofed painted canvas on the exterior and dyed canvas on the interior.[43] This type of construction was found to be both economical and aesthetically pleasing. The canvas could be brought flush with door and window frames, eliminating the need for trim pieces.

If these houses had been mass-produced, prefabricated steel components would have been employed, with canvas stretched over a combination of insulation board and aluminum foil for insulation. Both houses were similar in concept: rectangles floating above the ground plane. Visually, the smaller house was a pure, solid object suspended in space, entered by a retractable folding stairway in the carport so that the means of entry was not obvious. The Experimental Five Room House also floated above the landscape, but it was not as functional as the Experimental Week-end House, as there was no carport below. It sat only two feet above the ground plane and had a long, narrow deck and stairs cantilevering off the front of the house into the landscape. By freeing the house from the ground plane, a tension was created that defined the volume of the house in contrast to the landscape.

Although neither house was built, the Cotton-Textile Institute used them as prototypes to demonstrate the possibilities of canvas as an important material for building construction.[44] The houses also served as a catalyst for Kocher and Frey's later work, the Experimental Week-end House providing the basis for Kocher's Canvas Week-end House (1934). Canvas was a familiar material to Frey; he had built canoes with it in his youth and had previously proposed a Miniature Golf Course [fig. 2.51, project, 1930] covered with a canvas awning for year-round use. This idea had sprung from his observations of the canopies in front of many apartment buildings in New York made of steel pipe frames wrapped in canvas. On the Experimental Five Room House a similar canopy is used to define the front door.[45]

42 | Rosa interview with Frey, 16 November 1986.
43 | F. R. S. Yorke, op. cit., 184.
44 | "Canvas for Houses," *Architectural Forum*, December 1932, 26.
45 | Rosa interview with Frey, 26 July 1987.

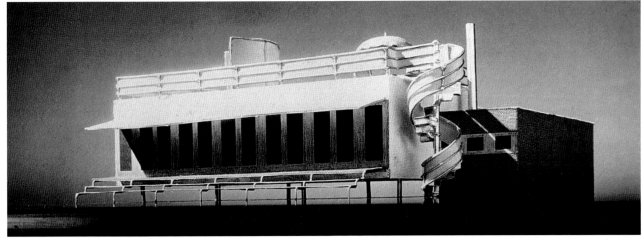

2.48

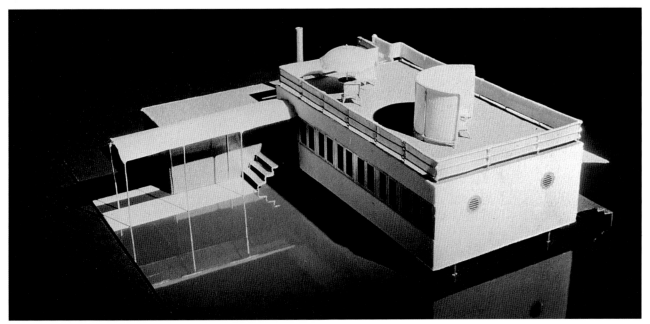

2.49

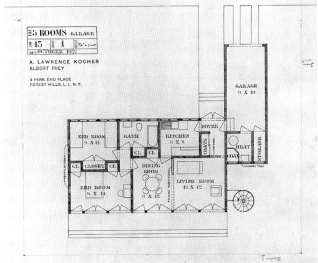

EXPERIMENTAL FIVE ROOM HOUSE, 1932

2.50

GUT-FREY HOUSE, 1933

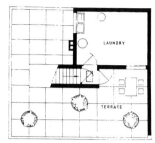

2·54

2·53

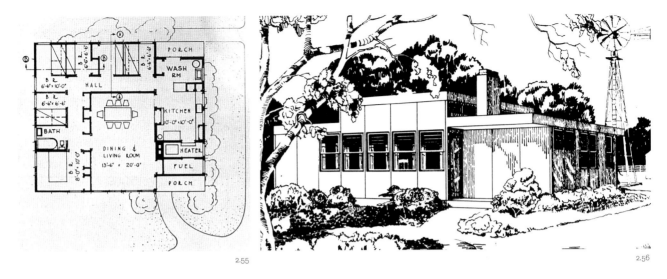

2.55   2.56

In January of 1933, Frey left Kocher and America for almost nine months to design and supervise the construction of a house for his eldest sister and her family in Zurich. His association with Kocher resumed shortly after his return to America. The Gut-Frey House [figs. 2.52–2.54, 1933], sited on a steep hill, consists of three floors with a roof deck. The ground floor has an open-air porch, an entry hall, and the utilities; the second floor has three bedrooms and a living room; the third floor has the kitchen, dining room, and a small apartment. A roof terrace was used for sunning and drying laundry. While supervising the construction of this house, Frey worked part-time, from March through October, for the architect Alfred Roth, a friend from Le Corbusier's atelier. En route back to America, Frey traveled with Roth to Paris to visit Le Corbusier and Jeanneret. He also went with Roth to meet Mondrian in his atelier, where he was impressed by the precise painting and immaculate studio; Mondrian's influence would later become evident in Frey's work when he began to break down pure volumes into planes.[46]

Three months after his return from Switzerland, Frey briefly moved to Washington, D.C., from January to March 1934, to work as a designer for the United States Department of Agriculture on its Farm Housing Project. The objective of this study was to create plans for low-cost farmhouses, which farm owners could request from the government. Of all the farmhouses illustrated in the *Farmers Bulletin No. 1738* [figs. 2.55–2.58, project, 1934], Frey's were the only modern flat-roofed ones sheathed with corrugated metal; all the others were traditional.[47]

46 | Ibid.; Alfred Roth to Rosa, 14 September 1988.

47 | Ibid.; United States Department of Agriculture Farmers Bulletin No. 1738, October 1934.

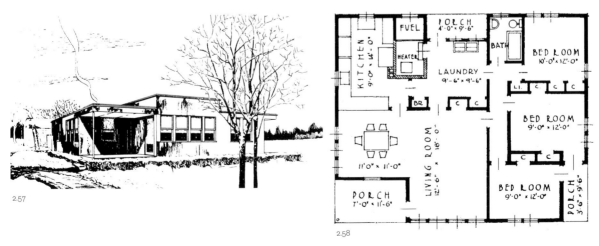

2.57   2.58

AMERICA, THE EAST COAST, 1930–39 : 41

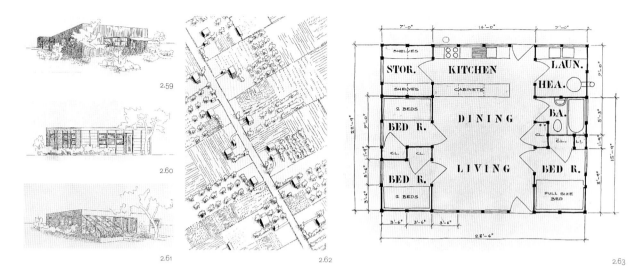

2.59: Metal Farmhouse

2.60: Precast Concrete Farmhouse

2.61: Concrete Block Farmhouse

Frey returned to New York in March of 1934 to continue his work with Kocher. One of his first undertakings was an article entitled "Subsistence Farmsteads" [figs. 2.59–2.63] for *Architectural Record*, in response to the Depression, when many people tried to supplement their incomes by growing some of their own food. The farmstead housing Frey designed was to be built on minimally sized lots and was neither intended to compete with commercial farms nor to provide total subsistence. The scheme was versatile and allowed the construction materials to change according to local conditions and availability. Concrete-block walls, precast concrete post-and-beam with concrete panels, or wood-frame construction sheathed with corrugated metal could all be used interchangeably. This flexibility had also been an important element of Frey's farmhouse designs for the Department of Agriculture.[48] The plan of the Subsistence Farmhouse is similar to Frey's Minimal Metal House (project, 1928) and to the first scheme for the Ralph-Barbarin House. The house combined the kitchen, living, and dining rooms in one common space, with private spaces around the periphery.

The idea of common living space was explored further with the Kocher Canvas Week-end House [figs. 2.64–2.71, 1934], where the common space was transformed into private space in the evenings. This house was constructed for Frey's partner, Kocher. The house was similar in design, but not in detail, to the Experimental Week-end House. Built in Northport, New York, about a mile from the shore, the house had three levels. The ground floor was used for the porch and garage while the roof deck was used for sunbathing and outdoor sleeping. Only the middle level was enclosed; access to it and to the roof deck was by an exterior circular stair. This second floor contained all the public and private spaces in one common area. A curtain track was mounted on the ceiling, and at night, drapes from the windows were pulled into the center of the house to divide the living room into bedrooms.

The Kocher Canvas Week-end House was supported by six steel columns that carried wood-framed floors and walls insulated with aluminum foil [fig. 2.64]. Diagonal redwood sheathing was coated with white lead paint immediately prior to the application of marine-treated canvas to bond it to the wood [fig. 2.65]. The canvas was applied horizontally, starting at the bottom of the wall, and was overlapped and nailed every six inches with copper-headed nails. It was then painted with three coats of oil-based paint prior to the finish coat. The interior walls and ceiling were veneered plywood with a canvas floor. The entire assembly required painting every three years.

Aesthetically, the Canvas Week-end House was a totally nonrepresentational object—the only thing that defined it as a house was its scale. It was constructed

48 | Frey to Rosa, 27 March 1989; A. Lawrence Kocher and Albert Frey, "Subsistence Farmsteads," *Architectural Record*, April 1934, 349–56.

KOCHER CANVAS
WEEK-END HOUSE,
1934

2.64

2.65

2.66

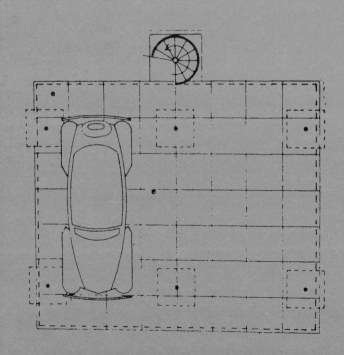
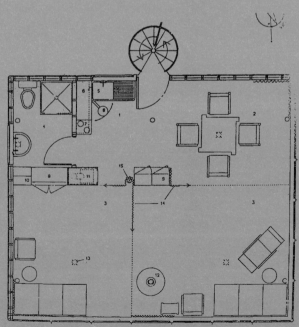

2.67

KOCHER CANVAS WEEK-END HOUSE, 1934

2.68

2.69

The envelope of the house is canvas and painted aluminum. Pipe railings and columns are painted sage green, as is the canvas roof deck. Steel sash windows and awnings are deep red. The interior walls and ceiling are plywood veneer; the floor is canvas and painted deep red.

KOCHER CANVAS WEEK-END HOUSE, 1934

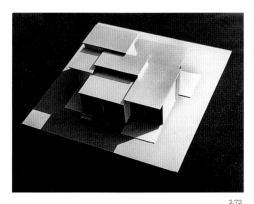
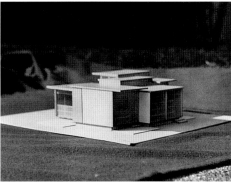

2.72 2.73

inexpensively, as the canvas was donated by the Cotton-Textile Institute to test its ability to be used as an exterior sheathing material.[49] It should be noted that marine-treated canvas was being used at the time as a roofing material for flat roofs and decks, and in the first edition of *Architectural Graphic Standards*, published in 1932, there were standard canvas roofing details guaranteed for five years. No one before Frey had taken this technology and incorporated it into the wrapping of an entire building exterior. The house withstood a hurricane in 1938 (although the trees around the house did not), only to be demolished by a developer in the late 1950s.[50]

As Frey became more interested in the concepts of prefabrication, standardization, and the use of industrialized materials, his designs began to reflect these concerns. A transformation in his work occurred as he began to break volumes into planes—a result of the new materials that Frey was using. In the House of Prefabricated Walls and Roofs, [figs. 2.72, 2.73, project, 1934] and in his West Coast work after 1940, this trend becomes obvious. Instead of a prefabricated panel system assembled on the site, as was the case with Farmhouses "A" and "B," Frey designed a prefabricated house in which each room could be completely assembled and sealed at the factory, brought to the site, and put together in less time than the farmhouses. Future enlargement of the houses could be indefinite.[51] This idea was an outgrowth of the Darien Guild Hall, where the size of each room was independently determined and the building as a whole was merely an assembly of different spaces. Formally, this later house became a series of parallel wall and ceiling planes at different levels that articulated the space of each room.

Frey and Kocher's next built commission, the Kocher-Samson Building [figs. 2.74–2.81, 1934–1935], was designed for Kocher's brother, Dr. J. J. Kocher, the first doctor to live in Palm Springs, California. The building housed a real-estate and insurance office on the first floor, with an apartment above. Photographs of the house were shown at the Museum of Modern Art exhibition *Modern Architecture in California* in October 1935, which featured the works of Kocher and Frey, Richard Neutra, R. M. Schindler, William Wurster, and A. C. Zimmerman. The Kocher-Samson Building was cited as being "typical of the restrained ingenuity of the eastern experimentalism which in contrast with that of California seems economical and chaste."[52] Kocher and Frey were the only architects in the exhibition who were not based solely in California; theirs was one of the first architectural offices to build on both coasts.

The Kocher-Samson Building is located on a long, narrow lot on North Palm Canyon Drive, the main thoroughfare of Palm Springs. Frey realized that the sites on both

49 | Rosa interview with Frey, 26 July 1987.
50 | Rosa interview with Marge Kocher, 15 September 1987.
51 | Rosa interview with Frey, 26 July 1987.
52 | Ernestine M. Fantl, *Modern Architecture in California* (New York: Museum of Modern Art, 1935), 3.

2.74

2.75

2.76

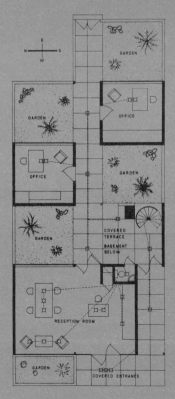

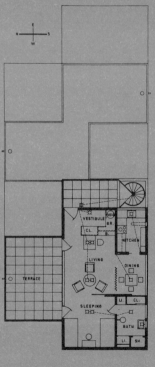

2.77

KOCHER-SAMSON BUILDING, 1934–35

The volume of the house is warm white with the walls
at the patio area painted sage green.

2.78

sides of the building would eventually be developed, so he designed the offices to overlook a courtyard. The first-floor plan is a large rectangle broken into smaller rectangles and squares based on a 3' x 3' grid. It contains individual offices and garden and terrace spaces wrapped by a high perimeter wall. A covered passageway acts as a central circulation spine, giving order to the assembly of squares and rectangles. At the second floor, the apartment is placed at a ninety degree angle, thus creating an outdoor terrace and overhangs for the offices below. The apartment is treated as a pure rectangle; elements built into the volume such as the kitchen, bathroom, and closets, are treated as separate entities from the rectangle, which is articulated by covering the secondary walls with plywood veneer and the perimeter walls with white plaster.

2.79

opposite: 2.80; above: 2.81

Construction of the Kocher-Samson Building used the latest available methods. The first floor was a poured-concrete post-and-beam system with concrete-block infill for the walls. At the second floor, the perimeter walls were of lightweight pressed-steel frames made in sections at the factory and welded together on the site. (The size of the prefabricated wall units was dictated by the size of the truck that transported the non-combustible materials the owner requested from the fabricator in Pennsylvania.) Four-inch-deep, keystone-shaped metal decking was used for all the floors and roofs. At the ceiling plane, the metal was exposed and linear light fixtures were placed between the recesses in the ribbing.[53]

At the end of October 1934, Frey left for Palm Springs to detail and supervise the construction of the Kocher-Samson Building. This was not his first trip across America; he had driven from New York to California in the summer of 1932, but at the time had not gone as far south as Palm Springs. He then stayed in Los Angeles where he met with and visited the works of Neutra, Schindler, J. R. Davidson, and Kem Weber. The Kocher-Samson Building was the last that Kocher and Frey would do together, although they collaborated once again in 1938. The dissolution of their partnership was amicable; there was no work in New York for Frey, and he had grown fond of the desert landscape and mountains, which reminded him of Switzerland. Palm Springs had become the new frontier for Frey; here he could be a pioneer with a raw landscape.[54]

Frey had met John Porter Clark (1905-91), his next associate, in California prior to ending his association with Kocher. Clark, one of the first architects to live and practice in Palm Springs, was born in Iowa, raised in California, and educated in architecture at Cornell University. All the work that Clark and Frey did together, from 1935 to 1937, was under the firm name of Van Pelt and Lind Architects, since neither Clark nor Frey was licensed at the time. Clark had worked for Van Pelt and Lind prior to attending architecture school, and they allowed him to use their name for his commissions.[55] Frey worked with Clark until April of 1937, when he went to work for Philip L. Goodwin on the project for the Museum of Modern Art in New York.[56] In 1939, he returned to the desert and resumed his partnership with Clark, which lasted for almost twenty years.

From March 1935 to March 1937, Frey saw eight of his projects to fruition. Most of them were done on a minimal budget. All were wood-frame construction with lath-and-plaster exterior finishes. None of these projects was constructed with donated materials, as both the Aluminaire and the Kocher Canvas Week-end House had been. During this time, Frey was trying to understand the landscape of the desert, its arid climate, and its

53 | Rosa interview with Frey, 16 November 1987.
54 | Ibid.
55 | Rosa interview with John Porter Clark, 18 October 1987.
56 | Frey personal papers.

2.82

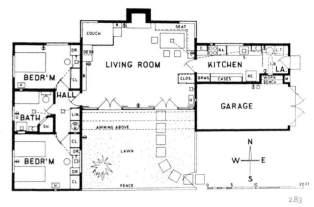

2.83

architecture. The Guthrie House [figs. 2.82, 2.83, 1935], the San Jacinto Hotel [fig. 2.84, 1935), and the Halberg House [2.85, 1936] all address the issues of the desert in different ways.

With the Guthrie House, he looked at the contextualism of the massing of the traditional adobe house and its relationship to the sun and shade; he used a stucco exterior to simulate adobe. Each function of the house was articulated as a mass, and there were no overhangs except for one large retractable canvas awning. The San Jacinto Hotel was Frey's first attempt to address mass housing on a small scale in the desert. Here, he used the Aluminaire as a prototype. Only three buildings were completed for the hotel, although it was planned as six units. Nevertheless, with this project Frey began to realize that a domestic-scaled volumetric mass without overhangs could not work in the desert. Covered porches had to be added to the building to block out the strong sun.[57] The Halberg House used such an overhang to deal effectively with the climate. Frey designed a planar roof that extended over the volume of the house and carport to shield the windows from the sun. The volume of the house was broken up in elevation by the articulation of the fireplace and windows.

57 | Rosa interview with Frey, 15 August 1987.

58 | Rosa interview with Clark, 18 October 1987; Rosa interview with Frey, 15 August 1987.

59 | Ibid.; James D. Kornwolf, ed., *Modernism in America 1937–1941* (Williamsburg, VA: Joseph and Margaret Muscarelle Museum of Art, College of William and Mary, 1985), 130, 196.

2.84

2.85

52 : ALBERT FREY, ARCHITECT

2.86

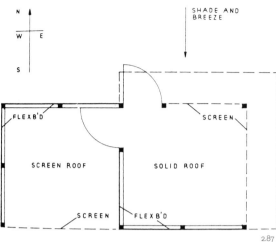
2.87

One of Frey's best buildings of this period is his smallest, the Brandenstein Study [figs. 2.86, 2.87, 1935]. Clark designed the main house and Frey designed a freestanding study for the owner, which was situated away from the main house for privacy. The study contains two square rooms: one has a solid roof that creates an overhang and the other has a screened-in roof. The walls are either asbestos-cement board or wire-mesh screen. This is one of the earliest buildings to demonstrate Frey's understanding of the the type of architecture appropriate to the desert climate; he would further explore and refine this type of building in his residential work of the 1940s.

Although modern architecture thrived in Los Angeles, partially due to the flourishing film industry, Palm Springs was still a virgin landscape. The only modern works built in the Coachella Valley prior to the Kocher-Samson Building were Schindler's Popenoe Cabin (1922) and Lloyd Wright's Oasis Hotel (1923). William Gray Purcell, a disciple of Louis Sullivan, built his own house in 1933, which he designed with Evera van Bailey, and to which Frey's Halberg House bears a strong resemblance.

Clark and Frey produced both traditional and modern work. If a client was receptive to modern architecture, Frey would design the building, but if a traditional or mission-style building was preferred, Clark would design it. This allowed both of them creative freedom and kept the office financially sound. When he was not working on modern houses, Frey would assist Clark with detailing and sometimes worked on the plans for his traditional California ranch and Spanish colonial homes. Clark, in return, would assist Frey with the details on the modern houses. Toward the spring of 1937, Frey found himself doing a larger proportion of traditional work. Fortunately, it was around this time that Frey was contacted by Philip L. Goodwin, who was working on a joint venture with Edward Durell Stone for the Museum of Modern Art [figs. 2.88, 2.89]. Goodwin needed a designer and asked Frey to return to New York. Frey, having worked on several schemes for the museum with William Lescaze, was a perfect choice. By May 1937, he was back in New York working for Goodwin.[58]

When Frey arrived, the museum was already under construction. He worked on design modifications of the street facade and subsequently designed the reading room, the lecture hall, and the typical flush-door and window details. He also designed two competition projects for Goodwin, both of which received third prizes.[59] The first was a Festival Theatre and Fine Arts Center for the College of William and Mary [fig. 2.90, 1938–39], for which Goodwin and Stone each designed schemes they submitted jointly. The other project was for the Smithsonian Gallery of Art [fig. 2.91, 1939]. Goodwin's

2.88

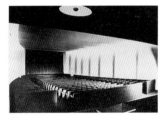
2.89

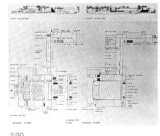
2.90

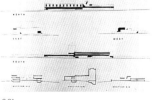
2.91

AMERICA, THE EAST COAST, 1930–39 : 53

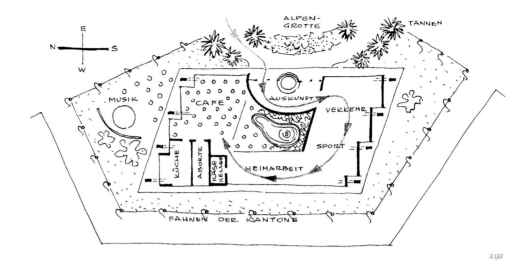

2.92

association with Stone had come to an end by that time, and the entry was submitted by Goodwin, Jaeger and Frey Associates. Goodwin offered Frey a partnership, and while they were negotiating, Frey wrote to Clark in Palm Springs to tell him the news. Clark asked Frey to return to Palm Springs to their partnership, as he had received his license and was now getting public commissions. Although Frey liked working with Goodwin and found him to be "open to ideas to an extent, but not as much as Kocher or Clark," he realized that this partnership would merely be a business arrangement and not a friendship as his collaborations had been with both Kocher and Clark. Frey decided to take Clark's offer. He left New York in July and drove across the country, arriving in Palm Springs in September of 1939.[60]

In New York in 1938, Frey had married Marion Cook, a writer he had met while visiting a mutual friend in Palm Springs. The marriage did not last, however, and they were divorced in 1945 because Frey would not compromise his need to be in Palm Springs, nor Cook hers to be in New York. Neither ever remarried. Prior to their divorce, they spent numerous weekends with Kocher and his family. During this period, in 1938, Frey collaborated with Kocher on a proposal for the Swiss Pavilion for the 1939 World's Fair in New York [figs. 2.92, 2.93].[61] The commission eventually went to William Lescaze, although Kocher did construct a project called the Plywood House for the World's Fair, but Frey had no part in it. During his time in New York, Frey published a book entitled *In Search of a Living Architecture*, with chapters on topics such as "The Evolution of Architectural Form," "Space," "Composition," "Form in Nature," "The Value of Traditional Architecture," "Modern Technics," and "Shaping for Human Needs." This book allowed him to explore his architectural ideas within the context of the American landscape, particularly the West. By this time, he had frequently driven across the country and had reconciled his design ambitions with regional climatic demands. The architecture that Frey would soon produce in the desert would have the same strength as his earlier East Coast work. He would finally be able to apply his Corbusian influence to a means of working with light and shadow in the desert.

60 | Ibid.
61 | Rosa interview with Frey, 30 November 1987; Marion Cook to Joseph Rosa, 18 April 1988.

2.93

The Evolution of Architectural Form

Form is the physical realization of an inner concept. Any individual form, therefore, is dependent on an intention and exists by the presence of a purpose. Experience shows that it continues to endure if the purpose continues. When the motivation, whether practical or spiritual, ceases or takes a new course, the form degenerates, decays, and finally disappears. Form variations and combinations are as countless as the thoughts that produce them. Generated by life, these efforts evolve with its evolution.

In the development of architectural form, first attempts concern themselves almost entirely with the bare materialization of an idea. Once this has been accomplished satisfactorily, attention shifts to the improvement of appearance. Creative expression reaches its climax when shape, space, and composition satisfy completely the practical requirements and interpret them in a design of intrinsic harmony.

The beauty such expression attains is one of clarity of shape, and the harmony that of balanced coordination. Significance and the pleasing proportion of form are closely related to physical reality. The dimensions of space or objects intended for human use are minimal, normal, or monumental in relation to one constant: the size of man. Mass of a building part, whether structure or partition, achieves good proportion when the material used determines the dimensions. Grotesque forms are apt to result when this principle is neglected.

Any externalization of a thought eventually comes to be accepted as a matter of course and creative interest in it develops toward the more subtle occupation of spiritual enjoyment. When this happens, the practical demands are often overlooked. If in the course of development, someone finds a better and timelier expression for them, the new solution tends to supersede the original form. The use that brought about the original remains as a connotation, but since we have dispensed with active participation in it, our appreciation becomes purely intellectual and emotional, a spiritual exercise or relaxation. Mental connotation, too, gradually diminishes, and when this is finally extinguished, imitation of the form, lacking the control of practicability, sinks into mere ornament, a hindrance rather than a stimulation to the development of idea and thought. This control of form is well illustrated in nature. Trees, streams, flowers, mountains all justify themselves in terms of purpose as well as of beauty.

Necessity dictates a skill in the original achievement of a form that cannot be duplicated by later imitators. The creative technique of our time goes into the production of objects derived from present conditions, not into the copies of traditional form. Continuation of conventional solutions that have become obsolete only retards natural progress in the establishment of expressive contemporary design. Acceptance of the inevitable change is slow because new designs demand intellectual effort while conventional patterns possess the advantage of familiarity based on habit.

Almost always the material element of an innovation receives immediate favor because it brings greater comfort, and adoption is not an effort but a convenience. For this reason, new products are often made desirable by preserving the old and customary appearance combined with the physical advantages of the modern development. Then step by step, the form is changed without the sudden break that would incur unaccustomed mental concentration. Finally people become used to and accept a new appearance that has evolved until it is fully expressive of the new media and conditions. Appropriate education and explanation of form evolution will speed up the process of assimilation and make possible the simultaneous creation of modern means and respective forms.

Often the attempt is made to compensate the lack of understanding of new shapes by terms that generalize the variegated aspects of modern products into an easily identified style, characteristic of some. When this happens, the result is faddish pattern superimposed on new objects indiscriminately. Discovery of newer possibilities and dissatisfaction with inappropriate adaptation force stylized fads into frequent changes, and the monotony which ensues from the unrestricted use of a fashionable form precipitates such changes into extreme reversals. Gradually, however, the most adequate expression of each product evolves and the individualized-shapes which result present stimulating contrasts that make general reversals unnecessary.

It is as much a mistake to transfer aspects of modern technics, without the presence of a similar problem, as to imitate the crystallized compositions of nature or old architecture. It is by studying the forms of nature, which have always inspired mankind, and those of traditional architecture, which have endured beyond practical usefulness, for theories of idea and structure that we will discover the basic principles which guide the creation of shape, space, and composition and be able to build a living architecture that not only provides us with physical comfort but with spiritual enjoyment as well.

From
Albert Frey, In Search of a Living Architecture *(New York: Architectural Book Publishing Co., 1939)*.

America, the West Coast, 1939–55

PALM SPRINGS IS a relatively small desert resort community that became incorporated as a city in 1938, the same year that airmail service was established. It wasn't until mid-1945, however, that regular flights from Los Angeles to Palm Springs began.[1] At the base of the San Jacinto Mountains, Palm Springs is located in the Coachella Valley of the Colorado Desert. Although the city is only about 125 miles from Los Angeles,[2] its desert climate is very different from the rest of southern California, and requires a very different approach to building from that of the East Coast or other areas of the West Coast. The temperature can easily reach 125 degrees Fahrenheit with zero precipitation, and severe sand storms often occur from March to June.[3]

Frey's work of the 1940s addresses the issues of sun, temperature, and prevailing winds. Using materials appropriate to the desert, from both a functional and an aesthetic point of view, he created a modern architecture that is firmly rooted in Le Corbusier's rhetoric but specific to the desert. His West Coast work therefore is radically different from the East Coast work: it had evolved from pure, nonrepresentational volumes raised off the ground plane to simple rectilinear compositions of planes that extend into the landscape. It also began to express the metaphor of the machine, due in part to the type of standard industrial materials available at that time.

Clark and Frey's buildings, both before and after World War II, were important contributions toward locating Palm Springs as a new frontier for the modern architectural spirit. Although relatively few buildings were built there before World War II, numerous architects drafted projects for this ideal resort community in the late 1930s and 1940s. One of the few to be completed was Neutra's first house in the desert, the Miller House (1938). Walter Gropius and Marcel Breuer, who were based on the East Coast, designed the Margoulis House (1938–39) for Palm Springs, although it was not executed because the clients divorced.[4]

While Hollywood was making movies that provided escape from the realities of the war, Palm Springs was entrenched in those realities. It was converted from a remote resort community to an army post and training ground, with strict restrictions imposed on civilians. The El Mirador Hotel, one of the first Spanish colonial revival style structures built in the desert, was transformed into the Torney General Hospital by the Los Angeles firm of Allison and Rible, for which Frey briefly worked in Palm Springs. He also worked for the Home Owners Loan Corporation, transforming stores and houses into apartments for the war workers' families; prefabricated classrooms were built for their children.[5]

1 | Thomas A. Jensen, "Palm Springs, California: Its Evolution and Functions," (M.A. diss., University of California, Los Angeles, 1954), 72.

2 | The Colorado Desert is in the Sonora Desert, which is part of the North American Desert; Collins H. Steere, *Imperial and Coachella Valley* (California: Stanford Press, 1952).

3 | Edmund C. Jaeger, *The California Deserts*, 4th ed. (California: Stanford University Press, 1965), 36.

4 | Winfried Nerdinger, *Walter Gropius* (Berlin: Bauhaus-Archiv; Cambridge: Busch-Reisenger Museum; Berlin: Gebr. Mann Verlag, 1985), 271.

5 | Rosa interview with Frey, 5 September 1987.

above: 3.1; opposite: 3.2

The influx of soldiers and their families led to a postwar building boom in Palm Springs and adjacent areas. Clark and Frey received numerous commissions for houses and commercial projects from war workers who decided to stay in the desert and start small businesses. One client of particular interest was Mary Nelson, who sold two-seater Ercoupe airplanes and gave buyers free flying lessons. In 1945, Frey designed a house (unbuilt) and store for her, and also bought a plane from her, which he sold after a short time.[6] After the war, Palm Springs reemerged as a resort community and several Los Angeles architects returned to building in the desert. Neutra sited his famous Kaufmann House (1946) on a lot adjacent to Clark and Frey's Loewy House; both were built by the same contractor. Schindler built the Toole House (1946) in Palm Village and John Lautner built the Desert Hot Springs Motel (1947).

The Frey House I [figs. 3.1–3.9, 1940], Frey's private residence of the prewar period, is the first house to exhibit his new interest in extending wall planes into the landscape, an idea he would further explore in his postwar residential projects. The walls of the house are a series of planes "frozen" by a large square roof plane that enforces the horizontal movement of the walls into the landscape and also acts as an overhang to create shade. In plan, the house is a 16' x 20' rectangle, comprised of 4' x 8' panels, and uses standard wood-frame construction. The walls extend into the landscape as screens to separate different outdoor activities, and they are as important in this function as are the interior walls for theirs. The envelope of the house is sheathed with corrugated metal, which is applied vertically to the static perimeter walls and horizontally on the wall planes extending into the landscape. All of the interior surfaces are colored asbestos-cement board fastened with screws. The light fixtures are incorporated into the walls and are covered with ventilation grilles to direct the light, in keeping with the compact nature of the design. The seating around the pool is embedded in concrete, thereby fixing the views framed by each seat and making them a part of the landscape.[7]

6 | Ibid.
7 | Ibid.

FREY HOUSE I, 1940

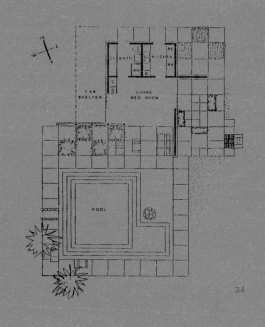

3.4

3.5

3.6

3.7

above: 3.8; opposite: 3.9

FREY HOUSE I, 1940

The asbestos-cement-board walls and corrugated metal ceiling plane of the Hatton House are painted shades of pale yellow and green to reflect the desert foliage. Window frames are painted terra cotta.

Frey further explored the idea of extending a building into the landscape in the Hatton House [figs. 3.10, 3.11] and adjacent guest house [figs. 3.12, 3.13, 1945]. The plans and volumes of these two houses are almost identical. However, the main house is an expanded rectangle in plan and the guest house is a square. The walls extend in four directions in such a way that the envelope of each house has been sheared and shifted.

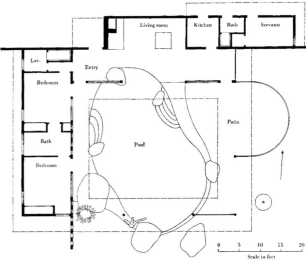

3.14

3.15

Again investigating this theme, Frey designed a house in 1946 for the industrial designer Raymond Loewy in which the walls become planes that define the points of entry [figs. 3.14–3.22]. The Loewy House consists of two long, narrow rectangles at right angles to each other which surround a pool that passes under one of the sides of the house. The only strong vertical element is the back of the fireplace, which denotes the entry, located at the intersection of the two rectangles. At this junction, the walls become static, and separate and differentiate the outside from the inside. On entering the house, one passes through another wall to find oneself "outside" again. To enter a room, one must again pass through one of the wall planes. The pool comes into the house, also blurring the distinction between the outside and inside. These elements break the boundaries of enclosure in the same way that the roof projects into the desert to claim part of the landscape as private space. Loewy contributed to the design of the house with pickled wood around the pool area, the interior furnishings, and the cosmetic streamlining of the living room ceiling.[8]

8 | Ibid.

3.16

AMERICA, THE WEST COAST, 1939–55 : 69

opposite: 3.17; above: 3.18

LOEWY HOUSE, 1946–47

3.19

LOEWY HOUSE, 1946–47

3.21

3.20

3.22

3.23 3.24

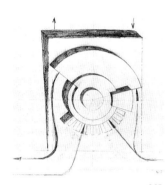

3.25

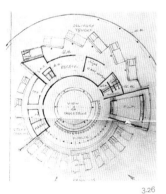

3.26

9 | Rosa interview with Frey, 31 October 1987.
10 | Rosa interview with Frey, 26 September 1987.

In contrast, the Woolley House [figs. 3.23, 3.24, 1945] is radically different from the Frey House I, the Hatton Houses, and the Loewy House. Here, the walls no longer act as horizontal elements moving under a strong horizontal roof plane. Instead, the horizontal roof plane is subordinated to the vertical wall plane, which has become a static element that defines the envelope of the building. Any walls that extend into the landscape become transparent screens. The roof plane is lower than the wall plane at the window areas, thereby creating overhangs.

While Frey was working with horizontal planes and movement, he was also exploring pure forms in the desert. His use of round forms started to appear as early as 1939, and he would continue to use them intermittently in projects like the Dellside Dairy (project, 1939), the Pellietier House (1951), and additions to the Frey House I (1947 and 1953).

Frey's proposal for the Dellside Dairy [figs. 3.25–3.28] consisted of a round building with a recessed central area for milk processing. A counter wrapped around this area so that visitors could sit and watch this process while eating. The building, which also contained a cinema, was adjacent to a highway, and was similar in concept to the drive-in food markets indigenous to California in the early 1930s. When Frey had traveled across the country in 1932, he had visited and photographed many of these buildings, and had been particularly impressed with Lloyd Wright's Yucca-Vine Market of 1928.[9]

In Frey's Pellietier House [figs. 3.29–3.31], a modern ranch house with rose-colored concrete-block walls and a pitched roof with shakes, one can see the influence of Frank Lloyd Wright's later desert projects that used circular forms and concrete block. Although this house is traditional, its siting is not. The house is curved, similar conceptually to Wright's Jacobs House (1943), and occupies a quarter of the circumference of a circle. A low garden wall continues the enclosure, with a pool and Washingtonia palm trees at the center.[10]

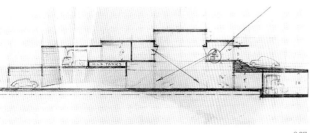
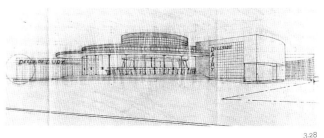

3.27 3.28

3.29

3.30

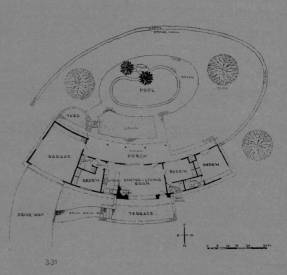

3.31

PELLIETIER HOUSE, 1951

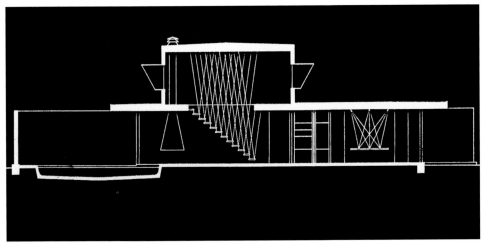

3.33

The Frey House I [figs. 3.32–3.42] is the most interesting and experimental of the three, however, since Frey used his own house as a laboratory to explore new ideas and materials. In 1948, he added a living room with an interior/exterior pool similar to the one at the Loewy House. His additions and modifications in 1953 transformed the house from a pure Miesian structure to an expressionist one—as David Gebhard has called it, "Frey's Flash Gordon" house. The bedroom added to the second floor is round in plan with round windows used to frame various views of the desert and mountains. To shade the windows, Frey designed individual awnings of sheet metal related to various angles of the sun; they wrap each window and give the effect from inside of looking out through a telescope. The windows pivot vertically at their center, and a semicircular horizontal bar locks them in place. The exterior of the round bedroom addition is sheathed in diamond-patterned rigidized aluminum; the interior walls are covered in yellow tufted vinyl fabric and the drapes are made of an electric blue vinyl, all giving this room a futuristic atmosphere. Other notable elements of the house include a stair to the bedroom addition and a round dining-room table, both of which are suspended from the ceiling with 1/4"-diameter aluminum rods. The outdoor pool area is enclosed by a curvilinear wall of corrugated fiberglass and metal.[11] Of Frey's many innovations in this house, both round windows and suspended stairs are used again at the North Shore Yacht Club (1958–59) and the Première Apartments (1957–58).

11 | Rosa interview with Frey, 1 November 1987.

opposite: 3.32; above: 3.34

AMERICA, THE WEST COAST, 1939–55 : 77

FREY HOUSE I WITH ADDITIONS, 1947 & 1953

Primary colors are used to contrast later additions with the rectangular original house. The bedroom is yellow tufted fabric with electric blue drapes. The exterior-interior pool, which faces west, has aluminum-faced drapes to reflect the sun. The pool enclosure (on the south side of the house) is corrugated metal with alternating ribbed fiberglass panels of red and yellow.

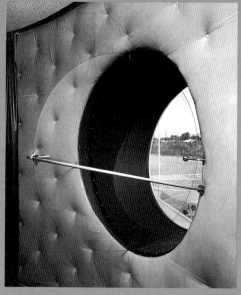

3.35

above: 3.36; opposite: 3.37

FREY HOUSE I WITH ADDITIONS, 1947 & 1953

3.39

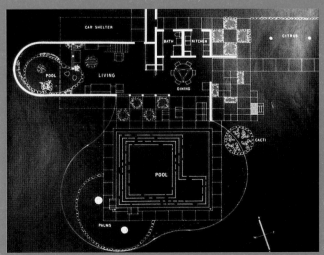

3.40

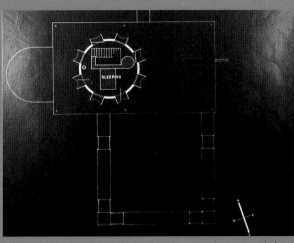

above: 3.41; overleaf: 3.42

FREY HOUSE I WITH ADDITIONS, 1947 & 1953

above: 3.43; opposite: 3.46

3.44

3.45

Although Frey's primary concern was with pure forms and abstract issues, he was also interested in the local vernacular architecture. Smoke Tree Ranch, a private resort community in Palm Springs, was the site of many Clark and Frey houses. The Ranch had a very specific design code that required all private residences to be built in a traditional ranch-style with a pitched shingle roof. In the 1940s, Frey designed two contextual houses there: the Markham House [fig. 3.43, 1941] and the Lyons House [figs. 3.44, 3.45, 1948–49], which both used natural materials and steel casement windows. Although the Markham House had a traditional pitched roof with shakes, it was modern in both plan and elevation. Frey differentiated the window zones from the solid wall planes by a change in materials: horizontal wood boards are used above and below the windows, but the wall area between them is stucco. The transition between these surfaces occurs at a vertical wood trim that extends from the window jambs on all the exterior elevations except along the patio area at the back of the house. The interior finishes are mahogany plywood and terrazzo floors.[12]

The Lyons House systematizes solids, voids, and planes within the idiom of the vernacular to an even greater extent than the Markham House. Its plan, similar to that of the earlier house, is open in the living and dining areas. The south wall consists of large glass sliding doors that open onto a private grassed patio and extend the house into the landscape. In plan, the patio, living, and dining areas read as one space. The house is articulated at the roof plane as three volumes organized around a patio: two of these volumes have traditional pitched roofs and the central volume has a split gable. This composition allowed Frey to frame the view of the mountains.

To break up the massing of the north elevation, Frey designed a series of three horizontal bands. The base of the wall is rusticated stone that projects past the face of the wall above and becomes a sill for the windows. The lower of the two bands of windows is the same height as the stone base; the space not occupied by windows is filled with vertical wood boards. The topmost band, the wall area above the windows, is of horizontal wood boards. The living-room window is the only element that breaks into that top band. Upon completion of the house, the Board of Directors of Smoke Tree Ranch found it to be too modern and banned Clark and Frey from building there for almost three years.[13] Despite this, Frey had shown that proportion and simplicity, within a traditional language, can create an elegant modern ranch house.

The Benoist Guest House [3.46, 3.47, 1950], built with fewer design constraints, is the best example of Frey's ability to deal simultaneously with contextualism

12 | Ibid.
13 | Rosa interview with John Porter Clark, 18 October 1987.

and modern ideology. With the Guest House, one can see his ability to site a structure equally well on a mountain or on a flat desert plain. But once Frey began building at the edge of and on top of mountains, the terrain necessarily forced him back to designing static, enclosed volumes. This later work does not have the plasticity of form of the earlier East Coast work, but it does have a far greater sense of materiality expressed in the volume of the buildings.

Rectangular in plan, the Benoist Guest House is a one-room studio with a bathroom and fireplace. Fieldstone is used for both the interior and exterior walls, while rocks from the side of the mountain pass through the fireplace wall. In siting the house to blend in with and relate to the mountain, Frey opened the volume vertically through the roof plane. The roof is all glass except in the bathroom, with a canvas awning that can be rolled over the top for shade.[14] Formally, the house is a stone box with no overhangs, the glass roof plane being stopped by the stone wall that rises above it. From a distance, it is reminiscent of an old stone house that has been abandoned for years, filled with memories of the past. The owner loved the spirit of the house and the quality of light so much that he made the guest house his office and rarely allowed guests to use it.[15]

Frey's interest in prefabricated housing never resulted in any buildings because the prefabrication of wall panels and rooms designed for minimum space and maximum efficiency became less viable. It never became feasible to produce the large number of units necessary to make prefabrication cost-effective, nor was it significantly more efficient than traditional construction techniques, particularly in California where construction could proceed year-round. The rise of modernism was slowed by World War II as both standard and experimental building materials became harder to obtain. And while the American economy was on the rise, the American modern aesthetic was being reevaluated: the image of the machine that was to bring a better life stood in sharp contrast to the negative aspects of new war technology. After the war, these attitudes changed and modernism, along with streamlined objects, became desirable again. But the interest in prefabricated housing continued to decline and was eventually replaced by the mass-production of mobile homes.[16]

During the war Frey designed two housing projects in Palm Springs, Bel Vista (1945–47) and Villa Hermosa (1945–47), but they were not built until the end of the war, due largely to cost issues. Construction for both was of standard wood frame with wood lath and stucco. Bel Vista was originally designed as war workers' housing by the Home Owners Loan Corporation; since its construction was subsidized by the government, it

14 | Rosa interview with Frey, 1 November 1987.
15 | Rosa interview with Mrs. Louis Benoist, 10 July 1987.
16 | Burham Kelly, *Design and Production of Houses* (New York: McGraw-Hill, Inc., 1959), 94–95.

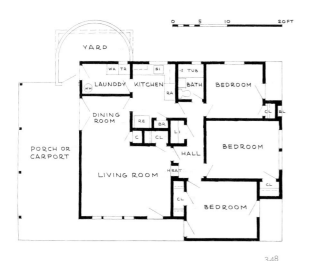

3.48

above: 3.49; opposite: 3.50

had to follow specific design guidelines.[17] Fifteen one-family units were constructed with one typical plan. Variations in their appearance were achieved by rotating and flipping the plan on each lot, thereby allowing various sides to face the street. In addition, each house was given individual identity by using different setbacks. A unique aspect of the plan is that each house has many entrances, through both private and communal spaces. This plan is almost identical to one of Frey's Farmhouse designs for the United States Department of Agriculture of 1934; both that project and Bel Vista sought to provide economical housing. Like most of Frey's earlier experimental housing, the Bel Vista houses allowed for future expansion, which many owners have undertaken over the years. One owner added to three sides of the house, finding the original plan very adaptable, with only minor alterations to the interior.[18]

The only similarity between Bel Vista [figs. 3.48, 3.49] and Villa Hermosa [figs. 3.50–3.54], designed the same year, is their concern with keeping costs down. Villa Hermosa was designed as a collection of apartments stacked and grouped around a pool and recreational facilities. Three separate unit types were designed, with the final building consisting of a total of twenty-one studio to one-bedroom apartments. The complex is a long, two-story, rectangular building flanked by two levels of individual units stacked irregularly to create overhangs and terraces. This assembly of stacked and terraced apartments forms a partial enclosure around a garden and a pool that is oriented to a mountain view—a continuation of Frey's earlier ideas, as exemplified by the Kocher-Samson Building. Access to all apartments is through the garden. Although the architecture uses the language of Le Corbusier's early housing projects, the placing of units around a green zone is an idea borrowed from the 1920s *Cité Jardin* movement in Brussels.

By 1940, Clark had become licensed and was able to obtain public commissions and upgrade the quality of the firm's projects to include schools and, later, larger commercial buildings. Frey became licensed in 1943, the first year the licensing board used a modernist architect—Richard Neutra—to review applicants. In 1957, Frey was made a Fellow (in design) of the American Institute of Architects.[19]

Another change in the partnership occurred in 1952 when Robson C. Chambers (1919–99), who had been an employee of the firm since 1946, was made a partner and the name of the firm was changed to Clark, Frey and Chambers. Chambers, born in Los Angeles and raised in Banning, California, received his Bachelor of Architecture from the University of Southern California in 1941. His role in the office was similar to Clark's.[20]

17 | Rosa interview with Frey, 1 November 1987.
18 | Rosa interview with Jim Louis, 26 April 1989.
19 | Rosa interview with Frey, 1 November 1987; A.I.A. document, Frey application.
20 | Rosa interview with Robson C. Chambers, 7 November 1987.

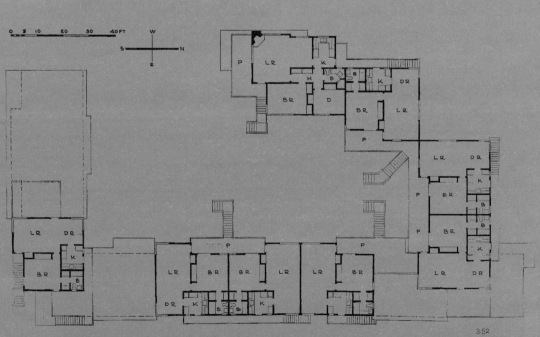

VILLA HERMOSA, 1946–47

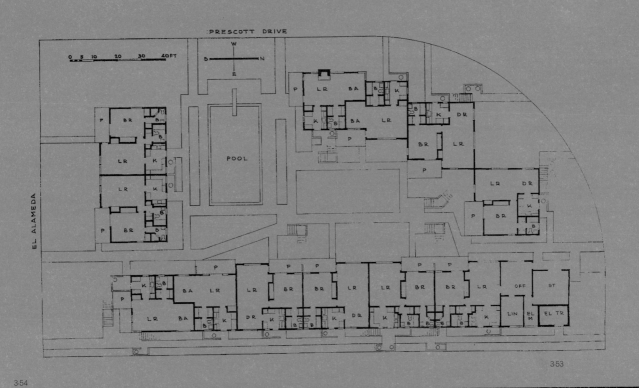

3.55

When Frey began designing schools, he created simple, cost-effective, modern, and functional buildings that addressed the arid climate of the desert. The Palm Springs Unified School District, which controlled all the schools in the Cahuilla Valley, did not advocate modern architecture, but chose to build modern schools because they were less expensive than the traditional Spanish colonial revival style ones.[21] Cathedral City, then a small farming community adjacent to Palm Springs, gave Clark and Frey their first school commission. The Cathedral City Elementary School [fig. 3.55, 1940], a simple, flat-roofed stucco box, consisted of one classroom with bathroom facilities.

The program for the second school, the Cahuilla Elementary School [figs. 3.56, 3.57, 1941] in Palm Springs, was formulated through faculty interviews. It expanded upon Frey's one-room school building to create a three-classroom, rectangular structure with an adjacent bathroom pavilion connected to the primary building by a covered walkway. The north wall is mainly glass, to bring in natural light and permit a view of the mountains. In addition, a long band of clerestory windows on the south wall provides light and ventilation. Frey designed built-in cabinetry around the rooms, and each room has an outdoor work area with storage cabinets and a sink.[22] The design of this building provided the school with a system that had the ability to expand indefinitely. By the early 1950s, Frey had added many more classroom buildings to the site, which were all identical in design to the original.[23] These additions were connected by a covered walkway that served as a circulation spine and shading device.

21 | Rosa interview with Frey, 30 November 1987; Rosa interview with Clark, 18 October 1987.
22 | Ibid.
23 | "Designed for Multi-Stage Construction," *Architectural Record*, January 1953, 117–23.

opposite: 3.56; above: 3.57

AMERICA, THE WEST COAST, 1939–55 : 93

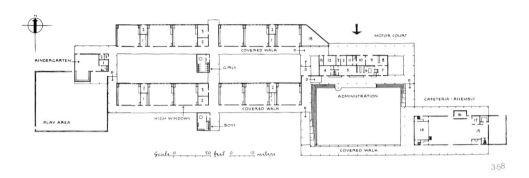

3.58

With the end of World War II, Palm Springs's population had almost tripled, and the need for schools increased. In response, the Katherine Finchy Elementary School [3.58–3.62, 1948–49]—the largest school that Frey had built to date—was erected in the northern part of the city. It had twelve classrooms in four separate buildings, an administration and cafeteria wing, and a kindergarten. To accommodate future expansion, the school was designed to be doubled in size by adding its mirror image to the southern end of the site. Although the component buildings of the school are rectangular, flat-roofed structures connected by a covered walkway, their siting is very different from that of the Cahuilla Elementary School. In plan, the Finchy School is a series of three squares, each edge of which is defined by a classroom pavilion, a parapet wall, or a covered walkway. By incorporating rectangular buildings into the established matrix of squares and

3.59

3.60

3.61

3.62

KATHERINE FINCHY ELEMENTARY SCHOOL, 1948–49

3.63

using the covered walkway as a circulation spine, outdoor spaces are created for classes and public assemblies.[24] Shortly thereafter, Frey was commissioned by the Needles Unified School District to build the Vista Colorado Elementary School [figs. 3.63, 3.64, 1949–51], which exemplifies his ideas for schools. Taking the elements of the Finchy school and expanding them through the use of new materials, Frey partially sheathed the Vista School in corrugated metal and used metal shading devices.

24 | Rosa interview with Frey, 30 November 1987; "Elementary School," *Progressive Architecture*, July 1953, 84–87.

3.64

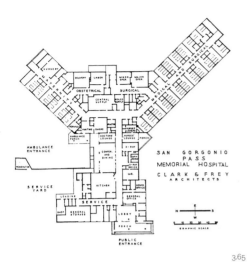 

3.65 3.66

Most of Frey's institutional work of the late 1940s and early 1950s consisted of one-story poured-concrete or concrete-block structures. A pure modernist example is the San Gorgonio Pass Memorial Hospital in Banning, California [3.65–3.68, 1947–51]. Functional concerns of the hospital shaped the basic form of the building: a pinwheel plan with two patient wings and one administrative and service wing, at the center of which are the surgical area and the nurses' stations. This plan minimized corridors and reduced travel distance for doctors and nurses.[25]

There are only two vertical elements in the design, both of which demarcate entrances. One, which displays the name of the hospital, is a concrete screen wall that passes in front of a projected entry overhang and penetrates the exterior wall. The other, the incinerator tower, is used to define the ambulance entrance. It is placed in the landscape at a short distance from the main building, but is visually connected to the hospital by a wall that divides this entrance from a service area.

25 | Rosa interview with Frey, 14 November 1987.

above: 3.67; overleaf: 3.68

SAN GORGONIO PASS
MEMORIAL HOSPITAL,
1947–1951

The exterior of the Desert Hospital is sandblasted terra-cotta-colored concrete block. Window shades and metal *brise-soleils* are painted sage green.

opposite: 3.69; above: 3.70

With the design of the Desert Hospital in Palm Springs [figs. 3.69–3.71, 1950–51], Frey incorporated the desert's landscape by creating an enclosed outdoor patio for patients to view the mountains. This space is adjacent to the lobby, but has convenient access to almost every wing of the hospital. The sense of the landscape is further enhanced by the addition of balconies to some of the private rooms. While both the San Gorgonio and Desert Hospital were designed for expansion, only for the Desert Hospital could this have been successful; a one-story building identical to the original one could have been built to the south and repeated three times, with the last unit consisting of two stories.[26]

26 | Ibid.

3.71

BANNING LIBRARY, 1954–55

The Banning Library [fig. 3.72, 1954–55], constructed with a poured-concrete frame, is a volumetric mass that Frey carved out in order to create overhangs and reveal forms. The recessed planes are either of brick or glass. A cylindrical shape identifies the children's area of the library, and is expressed both inside and outside the building. The ceiling plane within the cylinder is dropped diagonally to a height that relates to the scale of a child, and the perimeter of the cylinder is wrapped with bookshelves.[27]

These institutional buildings reveal the transition from Frey's earlier functionalist ideology to a more lyrical approach, a process that had already occurred in his residential works. This lyricism, which initially expressed itself only in plan, continued to grow and eventually emerged as an expressive sense both of plan and enclosure in the later institutional and commercial work.

27 | Ibid.

America, the Late West Coast, 1955–86

4.1 4.2

1955 MARKED THE BEGINNING of an important decade for Frey. In July and August, he toured Rome, Agra, Athens, Cairo, New Delhi, Bangkok, Hong Kong, and Tokyo where he visited Kunio Maekawa. While in India, he took a side trip to see Chandigarh and visit Pierre Jeanneret.[1] During this period, Frey's firm would receive some of its largest and most significant commissions in Palm Springs, and in the decade that followed, he would return to designing what he was most passionate about: houses.

When Frey returned from his trip around the world at the end of 1955, he completed the final scheme for one of his most important public buildings, the Palm Springs City Hall [figs. 4.1–4.6, 1952–57]. While traveling, Frey's interest in the relationship between pure form and function was renewed; this interest is reflected in the City Hall by the creation of a separate volume for the Council Chamber. The main volume of the building is linear and symmetrical, with a wing extending from the rear of the main entrance. To the right of this is the Council Chamber, which is higher than the rest of the building; the functional requirements of a public assembly hall were used to shape the space. All of its perimeter exterior walls are stepped to improve the acoustics and to bring in north light. A *brise-soleil* serves as a covered walkway between the two volumes and anchors the Council Chamber to the main building, thereby creating an overall asymmetrical composition in plan. The entrance to the Council Chamber is more elaborate than the main entrance. A sign above it states that "The People Are The City," and it is marked by a poured-concrete disk held up by four columns. This disk corresponds to the void left by a circle removed from the rectangular metal plane that marks the main entry. The building is constructed of concrete blocks, every two rows of which are aligned, thereby creating a pattern of squares in elevation. The metal overhangs and the metal *brise-soleils* are made up of a series of shallow sheet-metal cylinders.[2]

The partnership of Clark, Frey and Chambers was dissolved at the end of 1956, the most lucrative year of Frey and Clark's nineteen years together. When Clark left the firm, the name was changed to Frey and Chambers. Clark, who had dealt with the business aspects of the firm, wanted to concentrate more on large commercial, public, and institutional structures at the expense of residential work. Frey, however, was interested in designing a variety of structures.[3] During the partnership of Frey and Chambers, their larger buildings developed a greater fluidity, with each project expressive of its function. The residential work also changed at this point. While Frey was still exploring experimental housing issues on a small scale, he began to infuse his buildings with metaphors specific to each project.

1 | Rosa interview with Frey, 1 November 1987.
2 | Ibid.
3 | Rosa interview with John Porter Clark, 18 October 1987; interview with Robson Chambers, 7 November 1987.

PALM SPRINGS CITY HALL, 1952–57

The exterior of the building is sandblasted terra-cotta-colored concrete block.
Window shades and metal *brise-soleils* are painted sage green.

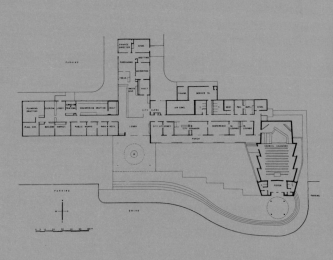

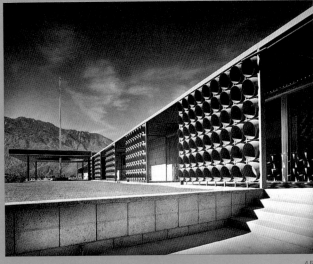

4-4

4-5

4-6

CREE HOUSE II, 1952–57

4.9   4.10

The Cree House II [figs. 4.6–4.9, 1955–56] exemplifies this change in Frey's residential work. It is a simple rectangle partially supported by pilotis. The fireplace, the only strong vertical element, passes through the horizontal mass of the house, cuts the corner off, and anchors it to a hill. The house is constructed entirely of industrial materials except for the stone fireplace, which relates it directly to the site. The house sits on the top of a rocky knoll and overlooks a great expanse of land and a road that still bears the owner's name. It does not represent the first occasion Frey had worked on this site, as Cree had commissioned him in 1947 to design the Desert Hills Hotel [fig. 4.10, project][4]—an unbuilt project of nine houses located along the natural contours of the mountain, with a large restaurant at the base. Eight of the private buildings had large cantilevered decks and were of the same plan, which was either flipped or rotated on each site. The last house at the top of the hill had a different plan and was nestled into the mountain, similar in site to the Benoist House. In contrast to Frey's earlier vision, the Cree House II was placed at the far edge of the mountain and balanced in place with steel columns; it was sheathed in sage green asbestos-cement board with yellow fiberglass panels enclosing the deck.

Around 1958, Romanoff's on the Rocks, a restaurant designed by the Los Angeles architect A. Quincy Jones, was constructed on the site where Frey had proposed the restaurant for Cree. Romanoff's was a flat-roofed, cantilevered, steel structure, and, with the Cree House II perched above it, presented a perfect example of 1950s California modernism in the desert. If the Benoist Guest House blended into the landscape, projecting an image of an old stone house with a few modern innovations, the Cree House II, in contrast, made no references to the past, but looked only to the future.

4 | Rosa interview with Frey, 21 November 1987.

4.11

4.12

4.13

As the years passed, Frey's ability grew to site residential works on the natural outcroppings of mountain sides and on their lower contours. Although not fully realized in his work of the 1950s, one can nevertheless see the genesis of ideas that would be successfully executed in the 1960s. In the Carey House [figs. 4.11, 4.12, 1956], Frey gave the client the "average suburban house" that she had requested, yet still respected the unique natural formation of the land. This interaction between two seemingly dissimilar concerns created an unusual building. The house is built at various levels above the ground plane, providing a ground-level carport and exposing the rocks and boulders that cover most of the site. Changes in elevation, expressed in the building volume, occur only at the floor plane; the roof is sloped to accommodate the various ceiling heights that result.

While the structure superficially resembles the quintessential suburban house, on closer observation, it becomes apparent that it is an assembly of industrial materials that needs no maintenance. The exterior walls are sheathed with asbestos-cement board fastened with exposed screws. The windows are steel sash casement and, as in the Markham House, the window zone is differentiated from the wall zone by the use of colored asbestos-cement board. The house is a wood-framed building supported by steel columns, as were the Experimental Five Room House and the Experimental Week-end House of 1932. However, the steel columns of the Carey House are not vertical, but angled, to stabilize the house in the event of an earthquake and to create a two-car carport.[5] The only visual connection between the house and the ground, other than the angled steel columns, is a large exterior stair.

By 1957 Frey started to experiment with different materials for functional reasons, as seen in the Première Apartments (1957–58). Compared to the Villa Hermosa [fig. 4.13, 1945–47] and the San Jacinto Hotel (1935), which are also resort hotels with apartment units, the design of the Première does not adhere to a strong ideology. Unlike the other hotels, this building is successful in addressing the arid climate of the desert [figs. 4.14–4.16]. Using extensive overhangs and materials such as metal to reflect the heat of the sun, the Première does not require excessive air conditioning to cool it. Situated on the flat desert landscape with views of the mountains, a pair of two-story buildings are placed perpendicular to each other, close to the edge of the rectangular site. The buildings form an L-shaped plan, wrapping around a pool. The individual units are recessed into the overall volume, creating exterior corridors on the outer elevations and private balconies on the side facing the pool and mountains. A narrow, metal covered walkway spans the remaining perimeter of the rectangle, defining the private

5 | Ibid.

4.14

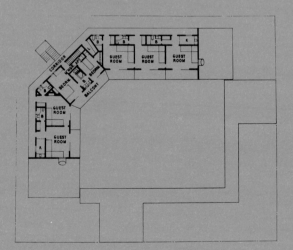

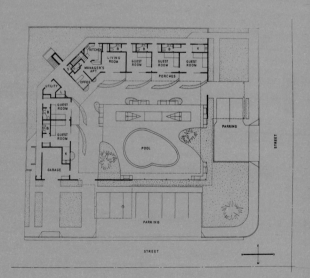

4.15

PREMIÈRE APARTMENTS, 1957–58

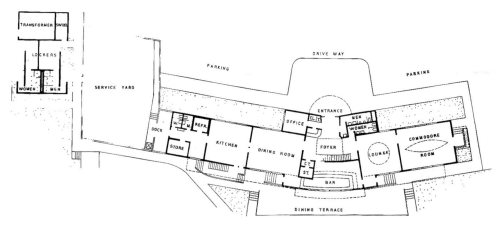

4.17 4.18

outdoor area. Corrugated metal planes extend from the covered walkway to cover parked cars.⁶ The layout is similar to the Chrystie-Forsyth Street Housing Development that Frey had designed for Lescaze some years earlier.

The Première Apartments combine concrete block, corrugated and rigidized metal, ribbed fiberglass panels, and plywood in one building. The shell of the building is sheathed in corrugated metal, the recessed exterior walls in grooved plywood. The railings and the vertical dividers between each balcony are covered with colored fiberglass panels. To minimize the use of exterior light fixtures and deck furniture around the pool, Frey designed stationary seating units made of concrete block that incorporated outdoor lighting.⁷ Several aspects of this building were derived from the Frey House I, the most obvious being the round windows at either end of the second floor wings, and details from it were to appear slightly later in the North Shore Yacht Club [210–214, 1958–59], the first commercial building that Frey designed after Clark left the firm.

With the North Shore Yacht Club in Salton Sea, Frey's work became more expressive and lyrical in both plan and elevation. This building, on the edge of the water, is a gentle curve with its convex side greeting the shore, reminiscent of the bow of a boat gently cutting through the water.⁸ The building's function is expressed through the literal metaphor of a ship. The second floor is sheathed in corrugated metal and is cantilevered over the ground floor, which is constructed of concrete block. This smaller upper floor, which resembles a crow's nest, accommodates a large lounge with four round windows that approximate portholes, and outdoor terraces with metal awnings that frame views of the water. Both the interior and exterior stairs leading to the ground level are curved and

6 | Ibid.
7 | Ibid.
8 | Ibid.

opposite: 4.16 **PREMIÈRE APARTMENTS, 1957–1958**

The building is wrapped in corrugated and rigidized metal with grooved plywood at the recessed wall of the balcony. Red, green, and yellow fiberglass panels separate the balconies from each other for privacy. The railings are covered with yellow fiberglass. The ground-floor private deck area is composed of low, curved, white fiberglass panels. Concrete block furniture is terra cotta, and the corrugated metal walkway that wraps and defines the outdoor space is sage green.

NORTH SHORE YACHT CLUB, 1958–59

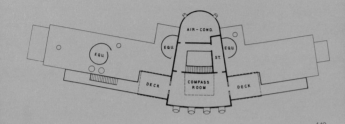

4.19

4.20

below: 4.21; opposite: 4.22

 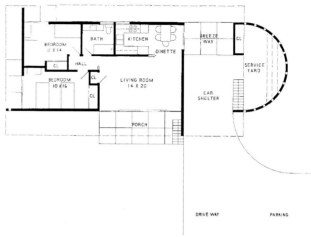

4.23   4.24

suspended, and, like many elements of the club, they are derived from Frey's early experiments with his own house. He also designed the North Shore Hotel adjacent to the Yacht Club, but prior to construction the design was modified against his wishes, and he did not consider the built version to be his own.

The setting for the Yacht Club was meant to be idyllic. The Salton Sea, a large body of water created from overflow of the Colorado River, is close to the Arizona border in the Colorado Desert, about three hours east of Los Angeles by car. In the late 1950s, developers intended the Salton Sea area to be a new, utopian beach resort where water sports could be enjoyed in the arid desert climate.[9] As several developments began to be built along the perimeter of the basin, reports were published indicating that expansion of development and agriculture would cause the water to rise in level and to become polluted by excess run-off. These warnings were ignored, and twenty years later this "idyllic" desert resort community had become a series of abandoned buildings surrounding a polluted basin where swimming was prohibited. At one point, the water level rose to the exterior dining terrace of the Yacht Club, almost surrounding the building, and ironically causing the boat metaphor to become a reality. By the late 1980s, the water level had receded, and the Yacht Club was used as a restaurant. However, efforts to revitalize the Salton Sea's North Shore quickly declined, and by the late 1990s the Yacht Club was left abandoned and looted. For Frey, designing projects for the Salton Sea "was a chance to build a new town that just did not turn out."[10]

A large subdivision called North Shore Beach Estates [figs. 4.23, 4.24, project, 1959] was to be located near the Yacht Club. Frey designed a house for this development, based on the principles of his early 1940s houses, with walls extending into the landscape. The walls were to be constructed of concrete block and capped with a strong horizontal roof plane that projected past the envelope of the building to create overhangs. The fascia and underside of the eaves were to be sheathed in corrugated metal. Frey added a semicircular wall to enclose an exterior yard for drying clothes, which was separated from the house by a breezeway that was to be used as a carport. The wall engaged the underside of the overhang and acted as a pure form supporting the horizontal roof plane.

If the development had been built, this house could have been used as a prototype, with variations created by rotating each house on the site to give it its own character. The house used ideas from Frey's earlier housing projects, but it was not intended as low-

9 | Mildred Stanley, *The Salton Sea: Yesterday and Today* (California: Triumph Press, Inc., 1966), 51.

10 | Rosa interview with Suzanne Sutton, Reference Coordinator, Palm Springs Public Library, 17 November 1987.

4.25

cost housing. When it was designed, Frey knew that constructing a house of concrete block would cost fifteen percent more than standard wood-and-stucco construction, but the development was to be promoted by assuring the public that concrete block was a permanent material that required no maintenance and was worth the additional investment. The concrete block also was in keeping with the language of the Yacht Club.[11]

Saint Michael's By-The-Sea Episcopal Church in Carlsbad, California [figs. 4.25–4.29, 1958–59] is also constructed of concrete block. The roof structure consists of laminated wood beams, and the roof plane is liberated from a horizontal line capping the plan to a series of angled planes that both define the volume and extend beyond it. The building thus becomes a composition of wall and ceiling planes free of rectilinear space. The highest point of the roof is directly above the altar, but in front of it is the sloped roof of the nave, which starts at a lower elevation than the sanctuary roof and thereby creates a clerestory that fills the sanctuary with light through stained glass. The roof above the sanctuary extends over the ancillary spaces and terminates at a steel-frame bell tower that penetrates the plane. Frey designed the nave of the church using the same method of angling walls to improve acoustics that he had used in designing the Council Chambers of the Palm Springs City Hall. The sanctuary is symmetrical in plan with the ancillary spaces at one side.

Saint Michael's was designed to accommodate a later addition, which might explain its awkward siting. The addition was to extend from the rear of the nave to increase the church in length. In such case, however, the view to the altar would have been partially obstructed. The church was designed to be seen from an automobile and to be experienced by foot only en route from the parking lot to the entrance, which is, therefore, oriented to the parking lot. The back of the church is consequently close to the edge of the property line, adjacent to the main boulevard. Because of the siting and the nontraditional design, many church members were concerned that the building did not look like a church and that people would not recognize it as such. In addition, the bell tower on the main boulevard was not perceived as a strong enough symbol for a church, so a sign was added to the boulevard facade. Although the church does not have traditional features, the interior has a sense of warmth, spirit, and light, which are achieved by the manipulation of the ceiling and wall planes, and while many members of the congregation were apprehensive about having a modern church they changed their opinions when they went inside.[12]

11 | Rosa interview with Frey, 21 November 1987.

12 | Rosa interview with Father John Woodridge, 3 August 1988.

4.26

ST. MICHAEL'S BY-THE-SEA
EPISCOPAL CHURCH, 1958–59

4.27

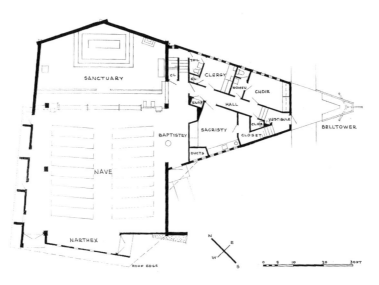

4.28

4.29

4.30

One of the best examples of Frey's thorough integration of architecture and structure is the Valley Station of the Palm Springs Aerial Tramway [figs. 4.30–4.32, 1949–63]. This commission was a joint venture of Frey and Chambers with Williams, Williams, & Williams, who designed the Mountain Station, and John Porter Clark, who acted as the coordinating architect. When it was built, the Tramway was the largest double-reversible passenger-carrying tramway in the world. Cable cars brought people from the Valley Station in Palm Springs to the Mountain Station, at an elevation of 8,516 feet on the slope of Mount San Jacinto.[13] Riders were transported from the arid desert climate to a mountainous area of pine trees and snow commanding a complete view of the Coachella Valley. Although the project was conceived in 1949, the actual design process began around 1960 and construction started in the summer of 1961. To adapt to the awkward site chosen for the Valley Station, Frey designed the building to rest on two plateaus that span a shallow stream flowing down Chino Canyon. The station was thus conceived as a covered bridge;[14] its walls are actually structural trusses spanning the two sides of the valley, and its windows reveal the structure of the trusses. The roof plane of the Valley Station is parallel to the slope of the land, which allows one to look up to the mountain and moving cable cars.

13 | Palm Springs Tramway pamphlet.
14 | Rosa interview with Frey, 29 November 1987.

4.31

4.32

PALM SPRINGS AERIAL TRAMWAY VALLEY STATION, 1949–63

4·33

Frey's exploration of the roof plane as a sculptural element is best seen with the Tramway Gas Station [figs. 4.33, 4.34, 1963–65], where he began to use more complex forms. The roof is a hyperbolic paraboloid and the plan is a truncated *vesica piscis*;[15] consequently, hardly any of the walls of the building are rectilinear. The roof plane spans more than ninety-five feet over the gas pumps and is supported by only six steel-pipe columns. It is constructed of ribbed galvanized steel panels resting on steel beams. The repair facilities were placed behind the building; therefore Frey needed to design a shape around which a car could easily maneuver.

The Gas Station, reminiscent of Erich Mendelsohn's expressionist sketches of the late 1920s and early 1930s, was designed to be a "sign" that could be easily read from a moving vehicle; it has a very strong presence and is the first structure one sees upon arriving in Palm Springs on Highway 111, the main road from Los Angeles. In a sense, it replaces a pair of simple, subtly curved stone gates Frey designed for the city in 1940, which no longer exist. The gas station, although recently threatened with destruction, still serves as a landmark at the edge of the desert and expresses the pioneering spirit of this resort community.

15 | Ibid.

4·34

124 : ALBERT FREY, ARCHITECT

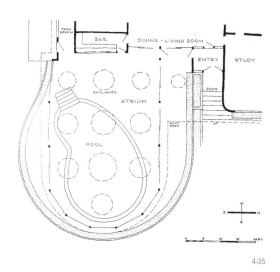

4.35　　　　　　　　　　　　　　　　　　　4.36

During the 1960s, Frey's projects grew in scale and he began receiving commissions from other southern California communities—Blythe, Beaumont, Indio, and Santa Ana. Other architects outside of Palm Springs such as Craig Ellwood, Victor Gruen, Pereira and Luckman, Paul Laszlo, and Welton Becket were also now receiving commissions in the desert. For Frey and Chambers, the change in the location and scale of projects caused the volume of their work to vary considerably from year to year, which, for monetary reasons, led to the dissolution of their partnership. Chambers was sixteen years younger than Frey and needed to support his family with a stable income. Frey had not remarried, had no children, and required less stability. After seeing their joint projects through completion, Chambers left Palm Springs in 1966 to work as a campus architect for the University of California at Santa Barbara. Frey moved his office to his house and took on only a few residential projects so that he could have more time to enjoy the desert.[16] Such a change in focus was already apparent with the Schiff House Addition at the Racquet Club in Palm Springs [figs. 4.35–4.37, 1960].

16 | Rosa interview with Robson Chambers, 7 November 1987.

4.37

4.38

FREY HOUSE II, 1963–64

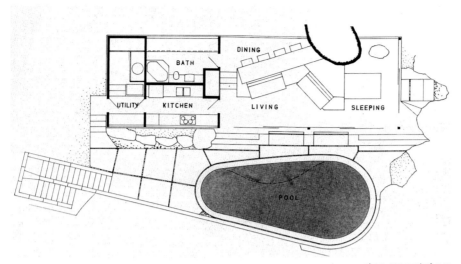

above: 4.39; overleaf: 4.40

In the later years of his career, Frey returned to simpler forms of structure and enclosure that further integrated houses into the landscape. Although these later houses are mostly pure structure wrapped in glass, Frey used the unique characteristics of each site to create spatial conditions that are contextual in a way his earlier East Coast work was not. The Frey House II [figs. 4.38–4.45, 1963–64] is his only built example of this adaptation of the modern idiom to the mountain terrain.

"After looking up at the mountains for almost twenty-five years," Frey once said, "it might be nice to live up there." The Frey House II soars 220 feet above Palm Springs and, at the time it was built, was at the highest elevation of any house in Palm Springs. (In 1973 the Hope House, designed by the Los Angeles architect John Lautner, was built across the valley and usurped this distinction.)[17] The Frey House II is located on a steep hill with natural rock outcroppings. A platform that is parallel to the road projects beyond the house and acts as a deck for a pool and as a roof for a carport below. The house, which is three steps higher than the deck, is on an east-west axis in relation to the rectilinear, man-made grid imposed on the desert below. The platform is placed in relationship to the natural contours of the mountain; the pool's teardrop shape is the result of the interaction of these two different orders.

The platform is constructed of poured concrete and colored concrete block to allow it to blend in with the mountain, and the house, which stands in contrast, is a pure rectangle with living, dining, and sleeping areas in one common space. Although the house seems at first to have no relationship to the site, it is actually firmly rooted in the mountain and interacts literally with the landscape. The elevation of the floor changes with the natural grade, and a large boulder penetrates the plane of the glass wall, anchoring the house to the site, much like the fireplace in the Cree House II. The ceiling plane is angled to accommodate the boulder, which acts as a focal point in plan, with each of the built-in cabinet units radiating out from it.[18] The house is of all steel-frame construction, with large spans of glass and colored corrugated aluminum on the exterior walls. The roof is enameled ribbed metal that blends in with the color of the rock. In 1972, Frey added a second bedroom, constructed of concrete-block walls and a steel-framed roof, to the west side of the house.

17 | Rosa interview with Sherri Abbas, Department of Community Development of Palm Springs, 19 May 1989.
18 | Rosa interview with Frey, 29 November 1987.

FREY HOUSE II, 1963–64

4-41

4-42

FREY HOUSE II, 1963–64

4-43

4-44

4-45

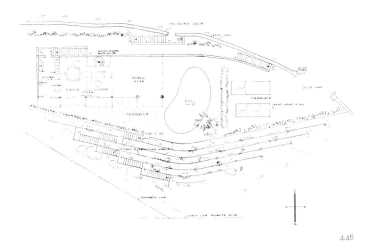

4.46

In contrast to the Frey House II, the Newton House [figs. 4.46, 4.47, project, 1966] projects off the edge of a mountain and almost becomes a floating object. The site was to be near the Frey House II, but at a lower elevation and at a steeper grade. The two-story structure with its lower level dug into the side of a mountain would have appeared, if built, to be one-story when viewed from the rear. A retaining wall on the lower level would have extended into the landscape, terminating in a stair to the second floor. The first floor, housing the common spaces, was opened to the site by means of a large plate-glass window. The retaining wall, which ran the length of the site, reinforced the feeling that the living areas and outdoor deck around the pool were one large, integrated space separated only by glass sliding doors. In contrast, the second floor's private spaces appeared to float above and dominate the rest of the house, while creating shaded areas below. Since the upper floor, supported by both pilotis and the retaining wall, appeared to be a solid, enclosed rectangle, the house did not necessarily read as a two-story structure, since one floor was open and transparent and the other was solid. By stacking the private spaces above the communal spaces, Frey used the narrow lot to accommodate a large shaded porch, a pool, and parking separated from the house by a hedge placed perpendicular to the retaining wall. The only biomorphic form was the kidney-shaped swimming pool.

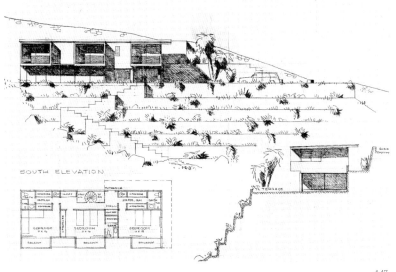

4.47

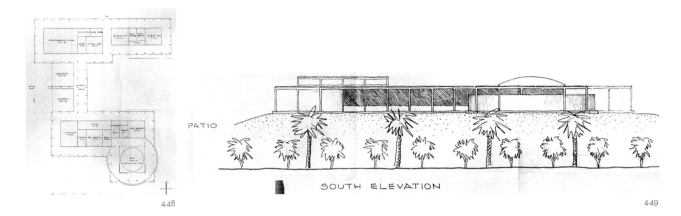

4.48

4.49

One of Frey's largest residential commissions was the Schiff Ranch House [figs. 4.48, 4.49, project, 1968], which included a main house, a separate guest house, and several office pavilions. Frey's design reduced the house, which was to have been sited on a flat parcel of land, to a pure machined object sitting in the desert landscape. By imposing a grid over the site, Frey created a complex program consisting of a lyrical composition of private pavilions within a matrix of covered walkways that act as porches and sun shades. The main house is separated from an office and guest pavilions by a covered walkway that also serves, in one area, as car parking. This carport, an integral part of the overall composition, becomes a fourth pavilion that reads as a negative space within the matrix. Here the client would drive a machine, the car, into an ordered grid of steel and machined parts defining both working and living spaces. Each pavilion is wrapped with a continuous walkway, and only an enclosed pool area would prevent one from walking completely around the complex without going into the sun. The pool, which is round in plan with a high wall surrounding it, was imposed on the ordered matrix of the building. The roof of the pool area was to have a shallow dome that would open electrically, allowing the pool to function as either an outdoor or indoor space. Although this project was not realized, it demonstrates the complete transformation that Frey's ideology had undergone since the early 1930s.

In the late 1960s, Frey entered into semiretirement, permitting him the option of choosing only challenging and interesting residential commissions. His late work consisted mainly of new houses at Smoke Tree Ranch and a few renovations to some of his earlier works; commissions in the modern idiom were few.[19] This, however, did not stop Frey from exploring new materials to support his ideas about what modern architecture in the desert could be—a formal typology that works within the arid climate.

In 1986, Frey was commissioned to build a house in the modern idiom outside of Smoke Tree Ranch. The Mirrored Pavilion [figs. 4.50–4.53], a collaboration with the owner, uses mirror (looking-glass mirror, not building curtain-wall mirror) as an exterior sheathing material. The owner was adamant about using this material in some way, so Frey investigated the material's properties and discarded traditional notions and connotations of the mirror, thus enabling him to use it as a sheathing material. The Pavilion is sited in a natural rock outcropping, with a large boulder penetrating one glass wall plane. In the interior, projecting from the boulder, a horizontal plane of glass serves as a table. The Pavilion is a steel-frame, polygonal structure and the ceiling is vaulted, with overhangs.[20]

The mirror that sheathes its exterior gives the house a somewhat surreal appearance. Looking at the Pavilion from afar, all one can see is a roof plane with rocks and

19 | Ibid.
20 | Ibid.

opposite: 4.50; above: 4.51   4.52

foliage beneath it and a narrow, horizontal band of windows imposed on the natural landscape. Only from a closer perspective does it become apparent that the rocks and foliage are merely a reflection of the site. Conceptually, the Pavilion is erased from the site, leaving only the roof as a trace of the shelter and the window as a trace of the view. Frey, always the pragmatist, saw the use of the mirror as purely functional: to camouflage the house and to reflect heat.

4.53

Albert Frey came to the United States filled with excitement about the modern spirit that was sweeping Europe. As the first architect to build in America who had worked directly with the modern master Le Corbusier, a new world was open to him. He was eager to explore the new technological frontiers that America promised, but found another frontier he had not anticipated—a virgin desert landscape that was his on which to build. Frey began his career by designing buildings in the language of the European modern movement—as static objects that stood independent from their sites—but he went on to create an architecture—desert modernism—that embraced the American culture of California, and invented an idiom of buildings that are machines for living in the rugged terrain of the desert landscape. American technology and its natural landscape had a very strong influence on Frey, and in turn, his architecture had a lasting impact on the development of the American modern movement.

AFTERWORD

SINCE THIS BOOK was first published in 1990, a renewed interest in California modern architecture has arisen, beyond figures such as Richard J. Neutra and Rudolph M. Schindler to other architects of the region. The history of the California aesthetic and its post-World War II adoption in Europe as a uniquely American West Coast idiom has been documented in numerous publications, most notably *Blueprint For Modern Living: History and Legacy of the Case Study Houses* (1989), edited by Elizabeth A. M. Smith; *An Everyday Modernism: The Houses of William Wurster* (1995), edited by Marc Treib; and *The Work of Charles and Ray Eames: A Legacy of Invention* (1997), edited by Donald Albrecht.

This renewed interest in West Coast modern architecture has expanded from Los Angeles and San Francisco to include areas such as Palm Springs. Albert Frey, who practiced in the desert from 1934 until his death, was a key figure in establishing the architectural idiom of desert modernism. In the past decade, a renewed interest in Frey's work illustrates how lesser-known figures in architectural history are playing a greater role in informing contemporary architects of ideologies outside the normative modernist canon. This same trend can be seen in a renewed attention to the works of other architects who until recently occupied the margins of California history, such as John Lautner, Gardner Dailey, Craig Ellwood, Pierre Koenig, and Joseph Esherick.

However, a number of lesser-known modern architects and designers still need to be studied to understand fully the magnitude of California's architectural production. As Esther McCoy stated in the introduction to her book *The Second Generation* (1984), "[T]here is much left to document [and]...I hope all bodies will be found while they are warm." McCoy's statement is still pertinent to the desert region of California. The careers of noted architects such as E. Stewart Williams, William F. Cody, and John Porter Clark (both his partnership with Frey, which set the tone for the practice of modern architecture in the desert, and his later work) remain to be documented.

Since the first publication of this book, various events of note occurred in Frey's life. In spring 1990, the Architectural Drawing Collection of the University of California at Santa Barbara Art Museum acquired most of Frey's personal papers (leaving a small selection of papers in Frey's own possession). After UCSB acquired the collection, I was asked by the late David Gebhard, Director of the Architectural Drawing Collection, to guest curate an exhibition on Frey. The exhibition *Albert Frey: Modern Architect* was organized in the same manner as this book, and opened at the University Art Museum in March 1992 with a symposium. Frey, however, did not attend; he had not traveled outside of the Cahuilla region of California since the late 1970s. The exhibition subsequently traveled to two other venues in the United States and three in Europe. It opened at the Palm Springs Desert Museum in September 1992, where Frey was able to see the exhibition. The exhibition opened on the East Coast at the Arthur Ross Architecture Gallery, Graduate School of Architecture, Planning, and Preservation, Columbia University in March 1993, in conjunction with another symposium on Frey. To coincide with the Columbia event, New York Institute of Technology, School of Architecture & Fine Arts in Central Islip, Long Island also planned an exhibition organized by Jon Michael Schwarting and Frances Campani entitled *The RE-Construction of the Aluminaire House and a visit to the HOUSE re-framing*. In 1995, *Albert Frey: Modern Architect* traveled to three venues in Switzerland: Architekturmuseum Basel in February; EPF Lausanne, Department of Architecture, in May; and ETH Zurich, Institut gta, in October.

These events—the book and exhibition, as well as the reconstruction of the Aluminaire House and the discovery of Palm Springs as a mecca for postwar modernism—have collectively brought the work and life of Frey to a broader audience and a younger generation of architects. Frey was rediscovered by the media, from fashion shoots that were set in his House II to features on him and his brand of desert modernism in magazines such as *Forbes, The New Yorker, Elle Decor*, and *Wallpaper**.

Frey's renewed visibility in the desert helped the Palm Springs community to recognize the value of its modern architecture. Today, Palm Springs has finally come into its own. Since the early 1990s the desert has been rediscovered by a culturally ambitious younger set that has infused it with a liveliness that had been lacking for more than twenty years. This growth of interest in mid-century modern architecture in Palm Springs is similar to the late 1970s discovery and preservation of Art Deco architecture in Miami Beach, Florida.

The younger set that has started to purchase homes in Palm Springs has been attentive to preserving its architectural character. The most noted recent debate in Palm Springs has been over the landmarking of Frey & Chambers's Tramway Gas Station that marks the entrance of Highway 111 into the town. The building was given landmark status, only to see that status revoked a month later. It was finally purchased by an enlightened businessman from San Francisco who learned of its imminent destruction through an article in *The New Yorker*; he plans to turn the defunct gas station into a sculpture gallery.

For most of Frey's decades in the desert he led a very private life, although he was a wonderful source of knowledge for many architectural historians. After the 1960s Frey's architectural vocabulary of corrugated aluminum, glass, and sandblasted concrete block became a less-acceptable idiom for new residential clients in the desert who

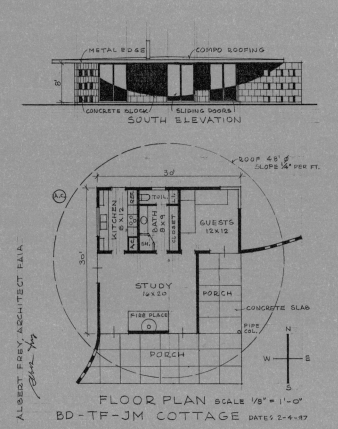

DUNNING-FORD-MOORE COTTAGE, 1997

desired the more traditional revival styles that were predominant in Palm Springs. At this point he became semiretired and worked on only a few select residential commissions, mostly located at Smoke Tree Ranch—where the idiom was California ranch.

Frey had designed houses at the ranch since 1941. By the mid-1980s, he was receiving commissions from the children of his earlier clients, mostly in the form of kitchen and bathroom modifications. Frey enjoyed these small projects, working with the contractors and visiting the sites on a daily basis. In one of our conversations I asked him how the ranch-house aesthetic compared to his own brand of modern architecture for the desert terrain. He simply responded: "It is an architecture that is true to its use of materials, versus Spanish revival with all that decoration, and I enjoy spending my day drawing and thinking about architecture." He slowly did less work at Smoke Tree Ranch, and by 1995 Frey had largely stopped doing any work there simply because the building department process had become too complicated and time-consuming.

By the mid 1980s—because of my original research for this book—Frey found himself again becoming a public figure and enjoyed a renewed dialogue with younger architects and designers. Most importantly, he was able to witness the next decade of vast interest in his architecture and his life. Frey had become equated with the modern idiom of the desert, and was a valuable source for many looking to understand the modern architecture of the Cahuilla region. He was consulted on the restorations of some of his earlier houses and intermittently sketched designs for individuals who were interested in his aesthetics. In 1997, Frey was commissioned to design a small guest cottage [z.1, z.2] for a hypothetical site by L.A.-based designer Brad Dunning; Tom Ford of Gucci; and Jim Moore, editor of *Gentlemen's Quarterly*. The program for this house was simple: minimal in square footage, affordable, and versatile. Unfortunately, the guest house was never realized, but it does illustrate that Frey's ideology never waned from his belief in a modern architecture for the rugged terrain of the desert.

On November 14, 1998, at the age of 95, Frey passed away of natural causes in his home (he is survived by his sister Emma in Switzerland). Although Frey never remarried, he had close friends who mark the decades of his life in Palm Springs. His Frey House II was bequeathed to the Palm Springs Desert Museum. The Museum hosted a public memorial in honor of Frey and his legacy in the desert, and he was buried at the Welwood Murray cemetery in Palm Springs.

Joseph Rosa, Alexandria, Virginia, 1999

BUILDING LIST

Albert Frey's projects and built works total more than two hundred. This listing is based on Frey's job lists from his various associations. I obtained most of the addresses by driving around the desert with Frey, locating the buildings or the places where they once stood, and recording their conditions. This occurred intermittently from June to December of 1987.

From 1930 to 1966, while Frey was in the United States, he worked in partnership with the following architects:

1930–35	**A. Lawrence Kocher**
1935–37	**John Porter Clark**
	(During this period all of the works by Clark and Frey were built and published under the name of Van Pelt and Lind.)
1938	**A. Lawrence Kocher**
1939–52	**John Porter Clark**
1952–57	**Clark and Robson Chambers**
	(During this period the firm also engaged in various joint ventures with Williams & Williams.)
1957–66	**Robson Chambers**

Frey worked as a designer in the following offices in the United States:

1931–32	**William Lescaze** (part-time)
1937–39	**Philip L. Goodwin**

The following list is comprised solely of buildings and projects that Frey was responsible for designing as a firm partner or employee. The list does not include all of the works of his partnerships with Clark and Chambers; it includes only those works that were designed by Frey and not buildings designed by his partners.

1925 **Frey Garage Addition** (project), Zurich, Switzerland
Furniture (project)
1927 **Concrete Parking Tower** (project)
Factory of Steel and Glass (project)
1928 **Furniture** (project/competition)
Housing for the Old (project/competition)
Minimal Metal House (project)
1929 **Office Building** (project/competition, placed second) [designed for Eggericx and Verwilghen]
1930 **Aluminaire House**, original location: Harrison Estate, 144 Round Swamp Road, Syosset, New York; new location: New York Institute of Technology, School of Architecture, Carlton Avenue, Central Islip, New York
Guild Hall (project), Darien, Connecticut
Master Plan of Bukavu, Belgian Congo (project) [designed for Eggericx and Verwilghen]
Master Plan of Uvira, Belgian Congo (project) [designed for Eggericx and Verwilghen]
Miniature Golf Course (project)
1931 **Chrystie-Forsyth Street Housing Development** (project), New York, New York [designed for William Lescaze]
Dodge Office Furniture (project), New York, New York
Downyflake Donut Shop (project), Rhode Island
Farmhouse "A" and "B" (project)
Museum of Modern Art, Scheme 5 & 6 (project), New York, New York [designed for William Lescaze]
River Garden Housing (project), New York, New York [designed for William Lescaze]
1932 **Experimental Five Room House** (project)
Experimental Week-end House (project)
Ralph-Barbarin House, near Stamford, Connecticut
1933 **Gut-Frey House**, Rebbergstrasse 41, Zurich, Switzerland [altered]
1934 **Cotton House** (project)
Farmhouses No. 6531 and No. 6532 for United States Department of Agriculture (project)
House of Prefabricated Walls and Floors (project)
Kocher Canvas Week-end House, Meadow Glen Road, Northport, Long Island, New York [demolished]
Kocher-Samson Building, 766 North Palm Canyon, Palm Springs, California [extensively altered]
1935 **Brandenstein Study**, 287 East Moronge Road, Palm Springs, California [demolished]
Guthrie House, 666 Mel Avenue, Palm Springs, California [altered]
San Jacinto Hotel, 726 North Indian Avenue, Palm Springs, California
1936 **Farwell House**, 2124 East Balboa Boulevard, Balboa, California
Halberg House, 687 East Vereda Sur, Palm Springs, California [altered]
Kellogg Studio, 321 Vereda Sur, Palm Springs, California [altered]
La Siesta Court, 247 West Stevens Road, Palm Springs, California [altered]
1937 **Mason House**, 448 Cottonwood Road, Palm Springs, California [altered]
Museum of Modern Art, 11 West 53 Street, New York, New York [contributing designer for the office of Philip L. Goodwin, a joint venture with Edward Durell Stone]
1938 **Festival Theatre and Fine Arts Center for the College of William and Mary**, Williamsburg, Virginia (project/competition, placed third) [designed for the office of Philip L. Goodwin]
Swiss Pavilion, 1939 New York World's Fair (project) [in collaboration with A. Lawrence Kocher]
1939 **Dellside Dairy** (project)
Chamber of Commerce (project), Palm Springs, California
Chaney Apartments, 275 Tamarisk Road, Palm Springs, California [altered]
Smithsonian Gallery of Art, Washington, D.C. (project/competition, placed third) [designed for the office of Philip L. Goodwin, submitted as Goodwin, Jaeger and Frey Associates]
1940 **B. Johnson Bungalows**, Palm Springs, California [altered]
Cathedral City Elementary School, Van Fleet Street and Second Street, Cathedral City, California [Frey additions 1947, 1951, and 1965; altered]
El Mirador Hotel Interiors, North Palm Canyon Drive, Palm Springs, California [demolished]
Frey House I, 1150 Paseo El Mirador, Palm Springs, California [Frey additions 1947 and 1953; unrecognizable]
Hill House, 877 Panorama Road, Palm Springs, California
Palm Springs City Gates, Highway 111, Palm Springs, California [demolished]
Skating Rink, South Sunrise Way, Palm Springs, California [demolished]
1941 **Cahuilla Elementary School**, 833 Mesquite Avenue, Palm Springs, California [Frey additions 1945, 1946, 1947, and 1955; demolished]
El Mirador Hotel, Shop Interior, North Palm Canyon Drive, Palm Springs, California [demolished]
F. D. Johnson House, Smoke Tree Ranch, Palm Springs, California [Frey additions 1973 and 1980]
Markham House, Smoke Tree Ranch, Palm Springs, California [Frey addition 1950]
Palm Springs Health Center, 459 East Amado Road, Palm Springs, California [unrecognizable]
Palm Springs Health Center, Palm Springs, California [demolished]
Palm Springs Water Company, 844 North Palm Canyon Drive, Palm Springs, California
Private House, 723 East Vereda Sur, Palm Springs, California [unrecognizable]
Sieroty House, 695 East Vereda Sur, Palm Springs, California
Simsarian Store, 824 North Palm Canyon Drive, Palm Springs, California [demolished]
1942 **American Airlines Terminal** (project), Palm Springs, California
El Mirador Hotel conversion to Torney Hospital, North Palm Canyon Drive, Palm Springs, California [for Allison & Rible Architects, L.A.; demolished]
H. Kellogg House (project), Phoenix, Arizona
Jaeger House (project), Palm Springs, California
Overly House, Smoke Tree Ranch, Palm Springs, California [Frey additions 1947, 1968, and 1983]
1943 **Home Owners Loan Corporation** [modifications to houses and stores for soldiers and war workers' families during World War II, in Palm Springs, Riverside, and Orange County]

1944 **Gilmore House**, Smoke Tree Ranch, Palm Springs, California. [Frey additions 1947, 1956, 1966, and 1977]
Home Owners Loan Corporation
Jacobson House (project), Palm Springs, California

1945 **Bel Vista War Housing**
1111, 1112, 1127, 1128, 1179, 1194 North Calle Rolph Road, Palm Springs, California [unrecognizable]
1133, 1149, 1164, 1165 North Calle Rolph Road, Palm Springs, California [minor alterations]
1163, 1193, 1132, 1180 North Calle Rolph Road, Palm Springs, California [altered]
1500 Paseo El Mirador, Palm Springs, California [minor alterations]
1520 East Tachevah Drive, Palm Springs, California
Breske House (project), Palm Springs, California
Browne Development (project), Palm Springs, California
Campbell House (project), Palm Springs, California
Cree House I, Hermosa Place, Palm Springs, California [demolished]
Doll House Restaurant, 1032 North Palm Canyon Drive, Palm Springs, California [demolished]
Florshine House Interior Alterations, 688 East Vereda Sur, Palm Springs, California
Hatton House and Guest House, Wonder Palms Road (now called Frank Sinatra Drive), Rancho Mirage, California [unrecognizable]
Kemper House Addition (project), Palm Springs, California
Nelson House (project), Indio, California
Nelson Studio, Monroe Avenue, Indio, California [unrecognizable]
Nichols Building, 700 North Palm Canyon Drive, Palm Springs, California
Powell House Addition, 383 West Vereda Norte, Palm Springs, California [Frey alterations and additions 1947, 1949, and 1951]
Racquet Club Bungalows, 2743 North Indian Avenue, Palm Springs, California
Strieby Apartments, 486–530 Mel Avenue, Palm Springs, California [altered]
Stutz Houses (project), Palm Springs, California
Van Heusen House (project), Yucca Valley, California
Woolley House, 856 Paseo El Mirador, Palm Springs, California [altered]
Villa Hermosa, 155 Hermosa Place, Palm Springs, California [Frey alterations 1948 and 1961]

1946 **Colgan Apartments**, 269 Chuckwalla Road, Palm Springs, California [altered]
Cooper House, 2360 South Araby Drive, Palm Springs, California
Cree Office Alteration, North Palm Canyon Drive, Palm Springs, California [demolished]
Desert Hot Springs Elementary School, Palm Springs, California [unrecognizable]
Loewy House, 600 Panorama Road, Palm Springs, California [minor alterations]
Lone Palm Court Addition, North Indian Avenue, Palm Springs, California [unrecognizable]
McFarland Apartment, 409 North Palm Canyon Drive (rear), Palm Springs, California [altered]
Nelson Guest House (project), Indio, California
Racquet Club Addition, 2743 North Indian Avenue, Palm Springs, California [Frey additions and alterations 1947, 1948, 1950, 1957, and 1961]
Samson Office Building, 760 North Palm Canyon Drive, Palm Springs, California [altered]
Seeburg Building, 1087–91 North Palm Canyon Drive, Palm Springs, California [altered]
Waale-Camplan Co. & Smith Inc. Office, Palm Springs, California [demolished]
Waale-Camplan Co. & Smith Inc. Office, Los Angeles, California
Zalud Stables (project), Beaumont, California

1947 **Clark & Frey Office Building**, 879 North Palm Canyon Drive, Palm Springs, California [designed with J. P. Clark]
Cree Ranch House (project), Palm Springs, California
Desert Hills Hotel (project), Palm Springs, California
Dollard Office Building, 687 North Palm Canyon Drive, Palm Springs, California [designed with R. Chambers]
Dr. Purcell Office Building Addition, 700 North Palm Canyon Drive, Palm Springs, California
Paddock Pool Co. Office Warehouse Building, 693 Ramon Road, Palm Springs, California
Rosenthal House (project), Palm Springs, California

1947 **San Gorgonio Pass Memorial Hospital**, 660 North Highland Springs Avenue, Banning, California [unrecognizable]
Stutz Apartments (project), Palm Springs, California
Willard Pool Addition, Santa Catalina, Palm Springs, California

1948 **American Legion Post #519**, 400 North Belardo, Palm Springs, California [designed with J. P. Clark; altered]
Cortissoz House, Sahara Road, Rancho Mirage, California
Desert Bank, 68–435 East Palm Canyon Drive, Cathedral City, California [altered]
El Mirador Hotel Restoration, North Palm Canyon Drive, Palm Springs, California [demolished]
Jennings House (project), Palm Springs, California
Katherine Finchy Elementary School, 777 East Tachevah Road, Palm Springs, California [extensively altered]
Lyons House, Smoke Tree Ranch, Palm Springs, California
Turner House, Smoke Tree Ranch, Palm Springs, California [Frey additions 1956 and 1986]
Wells House (project), Rancho Mirage, California

1949 **"D" Street Elementary School Addition**, Cibola Street and "D" Street, Needles, California
Essex Elementary School Addition, Needles, California
Palm Springs Tramway Valley Station, Tramway Road, Palm Springs, California
Tobin House, Port Angeles, Washington
Turonnet Building, 707–745 North Palm Canyon Drive, Palm Springs, California [altered]
Vista Colorado Elementary School, Washington Street and Bailey Street, Needles, California [extensively altered]

1950 **Benoist Guest House**, (address withheld at request of owner), Palm Springs, California [damaged by fire, restored]
Desert Hospital, 1150 North Indian Avenue, Palm Springs, California [extensively altered]
Palm Springs Fire Station, Ramon Road and Sunrise Way, Palm Springs, California [minor alterations]
University of California at Riverside Social Sciences & Humanities Building, Riverside, California

1951 **Dollard House**, 34–660 Mission Hills Country Club, Rancho Mirage, California
Joy House, 73–335 Grapevine Road, Palm Desert, California
Parker Dam School, Needles, California
Pellietier House, 73–297 Grapevine Road, Palm Desert, California
Turonnet House Addition, 734 North Prescot Drive, Palm Springs, California [extensively altered]

1952 **Cahuilla Elementary School Multi-Purpose Building**, 833 Mesquite Avenue, Palm Springs, California [demolished]
Palm Springs City Hall, 3200 East Tahquitz McCallum, Palm Springs, California [altered]

1953 **Benoist House Addition** (project), Palm Springs, California
Desert Museum, East Tahquitz Way, Palm Springs, California [demolished]
Nichols Building, 891, 895, 897, 899 North Palm Canyon Drive, Palm Springs, California

1954 **Banning Library**, 21 West Nicolet Street, Banning, California [altered]
Hinton House, 9420 La Jolla Shores Drive, La Jolla, California [altered]

1955 **Cielo Vista School**, 650 Paseo Dorotea, Palm Springs, California [altered]
Cree House II, 66–389 East Highway III, Cathedral City, California
Fire Station No. 1, 277 Indian Avenue, Palm Springs, California

1956 **Benoist House Addition**, (address withheld at request of owner), Palm Springs, California

1956 **Carey House**, 651 West Via Escula, Palm Springs, California [Frey alteration 1983]
Colgan Apartments Addition, 269 Chuckwalla Road, Palm Springs, California
First Church of Christ, 605 South Riverside Drive, Palm Springs, California [designed with R. Chambers]
Slaughter Office Building, 250 East Palm Canyon Drive, Palm Springs, California [unrecognizable]

1957 **Burgess House Addition**, 550 Palisades Drive, Palm Springs, California
Cree Site and Houses (project), Palm Springs, California
Foursquare Gospel Church, 630 Vella Road, Palm Springs, California [altered]
Première Apartments, original location: 150 West Baristo Road, Palm Springs, California; relocated to: 261 South Belardo Road [minor alterations]

1958 **Nellie Coffman School Multi-Purpose and Administration Building**, 400 South Cerritos, Palm Springs, California [Frey addition 1960; altered]
North Shore Yacht Club, 99–155 Sea View Drive, Salton Sea, California
Palm Springs High School Shop Building, 2248 East Ramon Road, Palm Springs, California
Saint Michael's By-The-Sea Episcopal Church, 2775 Carlsbad Boulevard, Carlsbad, California [designed with R. Chambers]
1959 **American Red Cross Chapter House**, 8880 Magnolia Avenue, Riverside, California
Frelinghuysen House Alterations, 707 West Panorama Road, Palm Springs, California
North Shore Beach Estates (project), Salton Sea, California
North Shore Beach Estates Sales Building, 99–155 Sea View Drive, Salton Sea, California [altered]
North Shore Beach Motel, 99–115 Sea View Drive, Salton Sea, California [not built as originally designed by Frey]
Ryan House (project), Bermuda Dunes, Palm Springs, California
1960 **Alpha Beta Food Market**, 81–731 Avenue 46, Indio, California [unrecognizable]
Alpha Beta Food Market, 755 North Sunrise Way, Palm Springs, California
Monkey Tree Motel, 2388 East Racquet Club Road, Palm Springs, California [not built as originally designed by Frey]
Schiff House Addition, Racquet Club, 2743 North Indian Avenue, Palm Springs, California
1961 **Clark House Addition**, Smoke Tree Ranch, Palm Springs, California [Frey additions 1965 and 1976]
De Anza Desert Country Club, Club House (project), Borrego Springs, California
Palm Springs High School Alterations, Palm Springs, California
1962 **Nichols Chino Canyon Hotel** (project), Tramway Road, Palm Springs, California
Nichols Restaurant (project), North Palm Canyon and Tramway Road, Palm Springs, California
Nichols Tramway Shopping Center (project), North Palm Canyon and Tramway Road, Palm Springs, California
Steinmeyer House, 318 South Pablo Drive, Palm Springs, California
1963 **Andreas Hills/Palm Canyon Ranch** (project), Palm Springs, California
Frey House II, 686 Palisades Drive, Palm Springs, California [Frey addition 1972]
Hollingsworth House (project), Palm Springs, California
Sillano House (project), Desert Hot Springs, California
Thorton House, Smoke Tree Ranch, Palm Springs, California [designed with R. Chambers; Frey additions 1969 and 1971]
1964 **Armstrong House**, Smoke Tree Ranch, Palm Springs, California
F. E. Supple House, Smoke Tree Ranch, Palm Springs, California [Frey additions 1967, 1976, 1978, and 1986]
Palm Canyon Mall (project), Palm Springs, California [collaboration with John P. Clark, William F. Cody, Richard A. Harrison, Herman Ranes, Roger and Stewart Williams]
Post Office, First and Murphy Streets, Blythe, California
Wahl House (project), Lake Tahoe, California
1965 **Graham House**, 1590 Via Monte Vista, Palm Springs, California [designed with R. Chambers]
Hi-Desert Memorial Hospital (project), Yucca Valley, California
Shell Oil Company, North Palm Canyon and El Alameda, Palm Springs, California [demolished]
Tramway Gas Station, 2901 North Palm Canyon Drive, Palm Springs, California [designed with R. Chambers; altered]
1966 **Brennan House Addition**, Smoke Tree Ranch, Palm Springs, California
Brennan House, Estherway, Jackson Hole, Wyoming
Hollingsworth House, 155 San Marco Way, Palm Springs, California [Frey additions 1972 and 1976; altered]
Lund House (project), Cherry Valley, California
Newton House (project), Palisades Drive, Palm Springs, California
1967 **Burgess Guest House** (project) 550 Palisades Drive, Palm Springs, California
Gilmore Guest House, Smoke Tree Ranch, Palm Springs, California
Smoke Tree Ranch Additions to Administration and Dining Room Building, Palm Springs, California
Smoke Tree Ranch Condominiums (project), Palm Springs, California
1967 **Newton House** (project), 698 West Ramon Road, Palm Springs, California

1968 **Nichols Store Building II**, 1200 North Palm Canyon Drive, Palm Springs, California
Schiff Ranch House (project), La Quinta, California
1969 **Thorton House Addition**, Smoke Tree Ranch, Palm Springs, California [Frey addition 1971]
1970 **Merwin House Addition**, Smoke Tree Ranch, Palm Springs, California
1972 **Goldman House Addition**, 1150 El Paseo Mirador, Palm Springs, California [Frey House I, 1940]
1973 **Moore House Addition**, Smoke Tree Ranch, Palm Springs, California [Frey alterations and additions 1979, 1983, and 1986]
Wasserman, Interior (project), Palm Springs, California
1974 **Ryan House**, Smoke Tree Ranch, Palm Springs, California
Siva Pool Pavilion (project), 200 West Vereda Sur, Palm Springs, California
1975 **Shane House Addition** (project), 501 Santa Rosa Drive, Palm Springs, California
1976 **Skelton House Addition**, Mountain Center, California
1977 **Beirne House Addition**, 395 South Patencio Road, Palm Springs, California
Lilley House Addition, Smoke Tree Ranch, Palm Springs, California [Frey addition 1979]
Phinny Guest House and Studio, Smoke Tree Ranch, Palm Springs, California
Terhune House Addition, 2300 Palermo Drive, Palm Springs, California [Frey additions 1978 and 1986]
1978 **Rose House Addition**, 1053 San Lucas Road, Palm Springs, California
Terhune Guest House (project), 2300 Palermo Drive, Palm Springs, California
1979 **Hankins House Alterations**, 840 Prescott Drive, Palm Springs, California
Hoffman House Addition, Smoke Tree Ranch, Palm Springs, California
Rawn House Addition, Smoke Tree Ranch, Palm Springs, California
1980 **Bryant House Addition** (project), Smoke Tree Ranch, Palm Springs, California
Phinny House (project), Smoke Tree Ranch, Palm Springs, California
Russell House Addition (project), 670 Palisades Drive, Palm Springs, California
1981 **Harpham House Addition**, Smoke Tree Ranch, Palm Springs, California
1983 **Burgess Guest House** (project), 550 Palisades Drive, Palm Springs, California
Lawrence House Addition, Smoke Tree Ranch, Palm Springs, California
Nichols Tourist Center (project), North Palm Canyon and Tramway Road, Palm Springs, California
Russell House Alterations, 660 Palisades Drive, Palm Springs, California [Frey addition 1984]
Smoke Tree Ranch Offices, 1800 South Sunrise Way, Palm Springs, California
Yantis House Addition, 296 West Hermosa Place, Palm Springs, California
Yates House Alterations, Smoke Tree Ranch, Palm Springs, California
Wilson House Additions, Smoke Tree Ranch, Palm Springs, California [Frey addition 1986]
1984 **Sherwin House Addition**, Smoke Tree Ranch, Palm Springs, California
1985 **Bauman House Alterations**, 1105 Cactus Drive, Palm Springs, California
Broderick House Addition (project), Palm Springs, California
Firring House Addition, 2065 Tulard Drive, Palm Springs, California
Green House Addition, Smoke Tree Ranch, Palm Springs, California
Shea House Addition, 1690 Ridgemore Drive, Palm Springs, California
Tyler House Addition, Smoke Tree Ranch, Palm Springs, California
1986 **Mirrored Pavilion** (address withheld at owner's request), California
1997 **Dunning, Ford, and Moore House** (project)

SELECTED BIBLIOGRAPHY

Writings on Albert Frey

1931

"Aluminaire—A New Departure in Residential Design and Construction." *American Builder and Building Age*, June 1931, 60, 61.

"Aluminum Instead of Wood House." *Boston Transcript*, 25 April 1931.

"Architect to Erect Glass Home For Self." *Brooklyn Daily Eagle*, 21 June 1931.

"Architects Show Modern Trends in Exposition." *New York Herald Tribune*, 18 April 1931.

"Architects' Show Visited by 100,000." *New York Times*, 26 April 1931.

"Architectural Art is Exhibited Here, All-Metal House Erected." *New York Times*, 19 April 1931.

"Architectural Show Has First 'Zipper House.'" *New York Herald Tribune*, 19 April 1931.

"A Community Art Center." *Architectural Forum*, April 1931, 465–67.

"Compact, Yet Comfortable, The Modern, Metal House." *New York World-Telegram*, 17 April 1931.

"Family will be All Bottled Up." *Los Angeles Times*, 21 June 1931.

Hambidge, Gove. "Castles in The Air." *The Country Gentlemen*, November 1931.

Haskell, Douglas. "The Architectural League and The Rejected Architects." *Parnassus*, 31 May 1931, 12–13.

"The Column, the Gable, and the Box." *The Arts,* June 1931, 636–39.

"Improved Lot Uses Recommended For Better Housing." *Real Estate and Builders Guide*, 27 June 1931, 5–6.

Jacquet, Lloyd. "Aluminum House at Architects Show Marks New Building." *New York Herald Tribune*, 19 April 1931.

Johnson, Philip. "Rejected Architects." *Creative Arts*, June 1931, 433–35.

Lee, William A. "The Aluminaire House: A Forerunner of the Glass Age!" *Glass Digest*, May 1931, 3.

Lohman, J. P. "Modern Home Built of Glass and Aluminum." *New York American*, 6 December 1931.

Lyon, Jean. "Housewife May Soon Order More Rooms by Telephone and Delivered by Parcel Post—Kitchen of Future." *New York Sun*, 23 April 1931.

McCormick, Elsie. "A Piece of Her Mind." *New York World-Telegram*, 21 April 1931.

"Plans Home of Aluminum and Glass." *Popular Science*, July 1931, 58.

Read, Helen Appleton. "Architectural League." *Brooklyn Eagle*, 17 April 1931.

Rice, Norman N. "Small House Construction—A Problem to be Solved." *Architectural Forum*, August 1931, 217–22.

"The Sun Dial—The All Metal Home." *New York Sun*, 23 April 1931.

Taylor, Deems. "Words and Music." *Brooklyn Eagle*, 18 April 1931.

"Two Years, Architecture." *Time*, 7 April 1931.

1932

"Aluminaire: A House for Contemporary Life." *Shelter*, May 1932, 56–58.

"Canvas for Houses." *Architectural Forum*, December 1932, 26.

"Functional-Type Buildings Shown." *Evening Star*, Washington, D.C., 27 December 1932.

Hitchcock, Henry-Russell. "Architectural Chronicles: The Brown Decades and the Brown Years." *Hound and Horn*, January–March 1932, 272–78.

Hitchcock, Henry-Russell, and Philip Johnson. *The International Style: Architecture Since 1922*. New York: W. W. Norton Co., 1932.

Hitchcock, Henry-Russell, Philip Johnson, and Lewis Mumford. *Modern Architecture: International Exhibition*. New York: Museum of Modern Art, 1932.

"Houses Made of Cotton." *The American Weekly*, 25 December 1932.

"Illustrated News, Model of Farmhouse of Low Cost." *Architectural Record*, May 1932, 297.

"Low-Cost Era Brings Us The House That Cotton Built." *Daily News Record*, 20 October 1932, 12.

1933

"Architects Show Modern Designs." *New York Evening Post*, 20 January 1933.

"Architectural Exhibition." *New York Times*, 21 January 1933.

"Foreseeing The Future of Architecture." *New York Herald Tribune*, 22 January 1933.

"Holzhaus in Stamford, Ct., USA." *Werk*, October 1933, 383–84.

"Inventions That Foster New Industries." *New York Times*, 5 February 1933, 8.

Keppel, Frederick P., and R. L. Duffus. "A House for Contemporary Life—The Aluminaire." *The Arts in American Life*. New York: McGraw-Hill, 1933.

1933 (con't.)

Sweeney, James Johnson. "Architecture, Old and New." *Creative Art*, April 1933, 272–73.

"Wood Framed House." *Architectural Record*, April 1933, 304.

1934

"Farmhouse Proposed for Lower Income Group." *Architectural Record*, April 1934, 346.

Johnson, Philip. "The Modern House." In *Art in America in Modern Times*, by Holger Cahill and Alfred H. Barr, Jr. New York: Museum of Modern Art, 1934.

"Low-Cost Farmhouse." *Architectural Record*, January 1934, 30.

McGrath, Raymond. *Twentieth Century House*. London: Faber and Faber, 1934.

"Modern Offices of Kocher and Samson Bring New Architecture to Village." *Palm Springs Limelight*, 15 December 1934.

"One Story Expansible Farmhouse." *Architectural Record*, April 1934, 344.

"Real Estate Office Building at Palm Springs, California for Dr. J. J. Kocher." *Architectural Record*, October 1934, 267–75.

"Week End House—Designed by A. Lawrence Kocher and Albert Frey." *Architectural Record*, January 1934, 34.

Yorke, F. R. S. *The Modern House.* London: The Architectural Press, 1934.

1936

Abercromble, Patrick. *The Book of the Modern House*. London: Hodder and Stoughton, 1936.

"Bedroom Interiors." *Architectural Record*, February 1936, 101.

"Casa De Week End En Estados Unidos." *Neustra Arquitectura*, October 1936, 386–87.

"A Community Exhibition Building Proposed for Darien, Connecticut." *Architectural Record*, December 1936, 425.

Editors of *Architectural Forum*. *The 1936 Book of Small Houses*. New York: Simon & Schuster, Inc., 1936.

Hand, Raymond B., ed. *Distinguished Houses of Moderate Cost*. New York: Robert M. McBridge and Co., 1936.

"House in Switzerland—Designed by Albert Frey." *Architectural Record*, July 1936, 35–40.

"Ralph-Barbarin House near Stamford, Connecticut," *Architectural Record*, April 1936, 296–97.

"Kitchen Apartment at Palm Springs." *Architectural Record*, October 1936, 318.

"Houses for Rufus Chapman, Guthrie and Mrs. M. J. Harrison, Palm Springs, California." *Architectural Record*, February 1936, 145–53.

1937

Edgerton, G. "Desert's Challenge to Home Builders; H. U. Brandstein and J. V. Guthrie Houses, Palm Springs, California." *Arts and Decoration*, August 1937, 19–21.

"Halberg House, El Mirador Estates, Palm Springs, California." *Architectural Record,* March 1937, BT26.

"La Siesta Residence Court, Palm Springs, California." *Architectural Record*, March 1937, BT16–17.

"The Palm Springs Home of Mr. And Mrs. James V. Guthrie." *California Arts and Architecture*, February 1937, 25.

"Real Estate Office and Apartment Building, Palm Springs, California." *Architectural Review*, March 1937, 114–15.

1939

Roth, Alfred. *The New Architecture 1930–1940*. Switzerland: Verlag Fur Architektur Artemis, 1939.

"Vacation House on Long Island." *American Home*, February 1939, 31.

1940

Ford, Jameds and Ford, Katherine Morrow. *The Modern House in America*. New York: Architectural Book Publishing Co., Inc., 1940.

McAndrew, John, ed. *Guide to Modern Architecture, Northeast States*. New York: The Museum of Modern Art, 1940.

Teague, Walter Dorwin. *Design This Day: The Technique of Order in the Machine Age*. New York: Harcourt, Brace & Co., 1940.

1942

"New Architectural Elements." *Architectural Forum*, September 1942, 124–27.

1945

"Two Desert Houses in Palm Springs, California." *California Arts and Architecture*, July 1945, 30–31.

1946

"Wohnhaus Albert Frey in Palm Springs, Kalifornien." *Werk*, June 1946, 202–204.

1947

"Desert House Blends Drama and Serenity, Glamor and Simplicity." *Architectural Forum*, May 1947, 62–64.

"A Small Modern House as Big as All Outdoors." *House and Garden*, May 1947, 78–83.

1948

"Apartments for Recreation, Villa Hermosa, Palm Springs, California." *Architectural Record*, February 1948, 116–19.

"House, Palm Springs, California." *Progressive Architecture*, July 1948, 63–67.

"A One Room House that Measures 16 Feet x 20 Feet." *House and Garden*, January 1948, 74–77, 102.

"Ranch House, Oasis at the Desert's Edge." *House and Garden*, March 1948, 106–107, 169.

1949

"Two Houses: Palm Springs, California." *Progressive Architecture*, December 1949, 65–68.

1950

"Architects' Office: Critique: Clark and Frey Architects." *Progressive Architecture*, October 1950, 60–62.

"Desert House." *Architectural Forum*, August 1950, 88–91.

"Desert Bank." *Architectural Record*, August 1950, 132.

1952

"Ferlenhaus in Palm Springs." *Werk*, June 1952, 187–90.

"Un ospendale a Palm Springs, California." *Domus*, July–August 1952, 12–13.

"La Scuola Nel Deserto, Clark e Frey Architetti." *Domus*, July–August 1952, 14–15.

1953

"Desert Bank Interior, Cathedral City, California." *Progressive Architecture*, June 1953, 128.

"Designed for Multi-Stage Construction." *Architectural Record*, January 1953, 117–23.

"Elementary School: Palm Springs, California." *Progressive Architecture*, July 1953, 84–87.

1954

Ford, Katherine Morrow, and Thomas H. Creighton. *The American House Today*. New York: Reinhold Publishing Corporation, 1954.

1956

Ringwald, George. "Palm Springs Octogenarian Builds New Home on Steep, Rocky Hillside." *Sunday Press Enterprise*, 30 September 1956, B5.

1958

Tripp, Vollie. "Living Architecture in the Desert Home." *Palm Springs Villager*, May 1958, 24–25.

1965

Gebhard, David, and Robert Winter. *A Guide to Architecture in Southern California*. Los Angeles: Los Angeles County Museum of Art, 1965.

1969

Banham, Reyner. *The Architecture of the Well-Tempered Environment*. London: The Architectural Press, 1969.

Gebhard, David, and Harriette Von Breton. *Kem Weber—The Moderne in Southern California 1920–1941*. Santa Barbara: University of California, Santa Barbara, 1969.

1971

Banham, Reyner. *Los Angeles, The Architecture of Four Ecologies*. New York: Penguin Press, 1971.

1973

Roth, Alfred. *Begegnung mit Pionieren*. Basel: Birkhäuser Verlag, 1973.

1975

Stern, Robert A. M. *George Howe: Toward a Modern American Architecture*. New Haven: Yale University Press, 1975.

1977

Gebhard, David, and Robert Winter. *A Guide to Architecture in Los Angeles & Southern California*. Santa Barbara: Peregrine Smith, Inc., 1977.

1978

Pommer, Richard. "The Architecture of Urban Housing in the United States During the Early 1930's." *Journal of the Society of Architectural Historians*, December 1978, 235–64.

1982

Hubert, Christian, and Lindsay Stamm Shapiro. *William Lescaze*. New York: Institute for Architecture and Urban Studies/Rizzoli International, 1982.

Wilson, Richard Guy. "International Style: the MoMA exhibition." *Progressive Architecture*, February 1982, 92–104.

Wodehouse, Lawrence. "Kocher at Black Mountain." *Journal of the Society of Architectural Historians*, December 1982, 328–32.

1984

Herbert, Gilbert. *The Dream of the Factory-Made House: Walter Gropius and Konrad Wachsmann*. Cambridge, MA: The MIT Press, 1984.

McCoy, Esther. *The Second Generation*. Salt Lake City: Gibbs M. Smith, 1984.

1985

Dunster, David. *Key Buildings of the 20th Century*. New York: Rizzoli International, 1985.

Kornwolf, James D., ed. *Modernism in America 1937–1941*. Williamsburg VA: Joseph and Margaret Muscarelle Museum of Art, College of William and Mary, 1985.

1986

Daly, Gail Ellen. "Architects Rally for Aluminum House." *Long-Islander*, Huntington, NY, 28 August 1986.

Fillip, Janice. "Architecture for an Arid Land." *Architecture California*, September–October 1986, 19–27.

Wilson, Richard Guy, Dianne H. Pilgrim, and Dickran Tashjian. *The Machine Age in America 1918–1941*. New York: The Brooklyn Museum/Abrams, 1986.

1987

Aguirre, Mary Lou. "Architect's Home Reflects Belief in Aluminum." *Desert Sun*, Palm Springs, 6 July 1987.

Benton, Tim. *The Villas of Le Corbusier 1920–1930*. New Haven: Yale University Press, 1987.

Goldberger, Paul. "Icon of Modernism Poised for Extinction." *New York Times*, 8 March 1987.

Gordon, Alastair. "Debate Over Modernist Ruin." *East Hampton Star*, 19 March 1987.

———. *Long Island Modern—The First Generation of Modernist Architecture on Long Island 1925–1960*. East Hampton, NY: Guild Hall Museum of East Hampton, 1987.

Gutis, Philip S. "It's Ugly, but So is the Fight to Save It." *New York Times*, 7 February 1987.

Hartocollis, Anemona. "Finding a Home for a Metal House." *Newsday, Long Island*, 18 June 1987.

Lanmon, Lorraine Welling. *William Lescaze, Architect*. Philadelphia: The Art Alliance Press/London and Toronto: Associated University Presses, 1987.

O'Neil, Maureen. "Masterpiece Slated for Demolition." *Newsday, Long Island*, 20 September 1987.

Rosa, Joseph. "First Metal House Future in Doubt." *Progressive Architecture*, January 1987, 31, 33.

———. "First Metal House Finds New Home." *Progressive Architecture*, December 1987, 25.

Stern, Robert A. M., Gregory Gilmartin, and Thomas Mellins. *New York 1930: Architecture and Urbanism Between the Two World Wars*. New York: Rizzoli International, 1987.

"Trying to Save A House of Metal." *New York Times*, 26 July 1987.

Vitello, Paul. "A Historic Pain in the Neck." *Newsday, Long Island*, 30 January 1987.

Wesson, Gail. "Architect's Mark is House of Aluminum." *Press-Enterprise*, Palm Springs, 5 August 1987.

———. "Desert Architect's Work is Saved from Demolition." *Press-Enterprise*, Palm Springs, 17 October 1987.

1990

Rosa, Joseph. *Albert Frey, Architect.* New York: Rizzoli International, 1990.
———. "A. Lawrence Kocher, Albert Frey, The Aluminaire House 1930/31," *Assemblage* 11 (1990): 59–69.

1991

Jandi, H. Ward. *Yesterday's Houses of Tomorrow: Innovative American Homes 1850 to 1950.* Washington D.C.: The Preservation Press, 1991.
———. "With Heritage So Shiny: America's First All Aluminum House." *The Journal of Preservation Technology* 2 (1991): 38–43.

1992

Jackson, Neil. "Desert Poineer." *Architectural Review*, September 1992, 40–44.
Leclerc, David. "Abert Frey: un moderne au desert." *L'Architecture d'Aujourd'hui*, February 1992, 130–43.
Riley, Terence. *The International Style: Exhibition 15 and The Museum of Modern Art.* New York: Columbia Books of Architecture/Rizzoli International, 1992.
Stieglitz, Maria. "A New Role For a Modernist Landmark: Students Restore Rescued Aluminaire House." *Historic Preservation News*, November 1992, 13–14, 29.
Tombesi, Paolo. "Conversazione con Albert Frey." *Casabella*, July–August 1992, 22–23.

1993

Rosa, Joseph. "Albert Frey: Modern Architect." *Newsline*, March–April 1993, 3.
Webb, Michael. "Desert Reflections." *Los Angeles Times*, 18 October 1993.

1994

"Albert Frey, Frey House II, Palm Springs." *GA Houses* 40 (1994): 34–43.
Magnuson, Ann, and Brad Dunning. "It's Back, It's Hot, It's Palm Springs." *Conde Nast Traveler*, September 1994, 159–70.
Rosa, Joseph. *A Constructed View: The Architectural Photography of Julius Shulman.* New York: Rizzoli International, 1994.
Stephens, Suzanne. "In the Thick of Frey." *Oculus*, May 1994, 4–5.
Trulsson, Nora Burba. "Palm Springs Modern California Architect Albert Frey Redefined Desert Architecture." *Southwest Passages*, May–June 1994, 42–49.
Webb, Michael. *Architects House Themselves.* Washington D.C. : The Preservation Press, 1994.

1995

Colomina, Beatriz. "The Media House." *Assemblage* 27 (August 1995): 64, 65.
Frampton, Kenneth. *American Masterworks: The Twentieth-Century House.* New York: Rizzoli International, 1995, 139.
Jackson, Neil. "Modernism pays homage to health," *Architects' Journal*, March 1995, 67.
Rosa, Joseph. *Albert Frey, Architekt* (with new introduction). Zurich: Artemis Verlags-AG, 1995.

1996

Forester, Kurt. "Albert Frey, de Robinson Crusoe van de Zwitserse architectuur." *Archis*, April 1996, 72–80.
Giovannini, Joseph. "Albert Frey in Palm Springs." *Architectural Digest*, July 1996, 42, 47–49.
Jackson, Neil. *The Modern Steel House.* New York: Van Nostrand Reinhold, 1996, 26–29, 30, 32, 36, 207, 214–15.
Ketcham, Diana. "Desert Swank." *House & Garden*, September 1996, 294–307.

1997

Haberman, Douglas. "Council Gets into Gas Station Fray." *Desert Sun*, 18 June 1997.
Jackson, Neil. "Favourite Buildings." *Architects' Journal*, October 1997, 55.

1998

Andersen, Kurt. "Annals of Architecture: Desert Cool." *The New Yorker*, 23 February–2 March 1998, 128–37.
Anderton, Frances. "A Desert Prophet Wins New Disciples." *New York Times*, 17 September 1998.
Cronstom, Kendell. "Elle Decor Goes to Palm Springs." *Elle Decor*, April 1998, 146–57.
Dial, Karla. "Modernist Architect Albert Frey Dies." *Desert Sun*, 15 November 1998.
Dunning, Brad. "Preserving the Optimism of Mid-Century Modern Design." *Los Angeles Times*, 28 June 1998.
Goff, Robert. "Modernism is Modern Again." *Forbes*, 7 September 1998, 256, 258.
Golub, Jennifer. *Albert Frey: Houses 1 + 2.* New York: Princeton Architectural Press, 1998.

1998 (con't.)

Goren, Manuela Cerri. "Palm Springs: Architectural Still Lifes." *L'Uomo Vogue*, May–June 1998, 108–13.
Iovine, Julie V. "Albert Frey, a Modernist and Minimalist Architect, Dies at 95." *New York Times*, 3 December 1998.
Jackson, Neil, Barbara Lamprecht, and Ruth Slavid. "Albert Frey, One of the Last H eroic Modernists. *Architects' Journal*, November 1998, 20.
Lamprecht, Barbara. "Frey's Frame." *Wallpaper**, March–April 1998, 37–40.
Liebrun, Jennifer. "Frey's Striking Work Revisited." *Desert Sun*, 22 December 1998.
Ourousoff, Nicolai. "Albert Frey, Modernist Architect, Dies." *Los Angeles Times*, 17 November 1998.
van Leeuwan, Thomas A. P. *The Springboard in the Pond: An Intimate History of the Swimming Pool.* Cambridge MA: The MIT Press, 1998, 290, 292.

1999

Book, Jeff. "Palm Springs Eternal." *Los Angeles Magazine*, April 1999, 69–79.
Colacello, Bob. "Palm Springs Weekend." *Vanity Fair*, June 1999, 192–211.
Cygelman, Adèle. *Palm Springs Modern.* New York: Rizzoli International, 1999, 19–33, 34, 44–51, 120–27.
Golub, Jennifer. "Passing: Albert Frey (1903–1998)." *Metropolis*, February–March 1999, 42.
Longstreth, Richard. *The Drive-in, Supermarket, and the Transformation of Commercial Space in Los Angeles, 1914–41.* Cambridge, MA: The MIT Press, 1999, 67, 129, 151, 153, 216.
Rosa, Joseph. Foreword to *Palm Springs Modern,* by Adèle Cygelman. New York: Rizzoli International, 1999, 16–18.
———. "A House for the Sickened World." *Casabella*, December–January 1999, 106–119.
Sirefman, Susanna. "Fast-Foward Frey." *Architecture*, January 1999, 56–59.

Writings by Albert Frey

1931

(with A. Lawrence Kocher). "Clothes Closets, Make them Convenient and Increase their Capacity." *Architectural Record*, March 1931, 237–43.
(with A. Lawrence Kocher). "Planning the House Garage." *Architectural Record*, January 1931, 52–57.
(with A. Lawrence Kocher). "Real Estate Subdivisions for Low-Cost Housing." *Architectural Record*, April 1931, 323–27.
(with A. Lawrence Kocher). "Stairways, Ramps, Escalators." *Architectural Record*, July 1931, 43–48.
(with A. Lawrence Kocher). "Windows." *Architectural Record*, February 1931, 126–37.

1932

(with A. Lawrence Kocher). "Design and Drafting Problems, Planning Offices for Economy." *Architectural Record*, September 1932, 197–202.
(with A. Lawrence Kocher). "Design and Drafting Problems, Seating Heights and Spacing Table Sizes and Heights." *Architectural Record*, April 1932, 261–67.
(with A. Lawrence Kocher). "Dimensions, Part One—Kitchens." *Architectural Record*, January 1932, 49–54.

1933

"Amerikanische Notizen." *Werk*, October 1933, 312–17.
"Gebrauchsarchitektur in U.S.A." *Werk*, October 1933, 382.
(with A. Lawrence Kocher). "New Materials and Improved Construction Methods." *Architectural Record*, April 1933, 281–89.

1934

(with A. Lawrence Kocher). "Check List for New Construction and Modernization of Houses Including Dimensions of Essential Equipment and Furniture." *Architectural Record*, February 1934, 123–28.
(with A. Lawrence Kocher). "Dimensions, Part Two—Bedrooms, Bathrooms." *Architectural Record*, February 1934, 123–28.
(with A. Lawrence Kocher). "Subsistence Farmsteads." *Architectural Record*, April 1934, 349–56.

1939

In Search of a Living Architecture. New York: Architectural Book Publishing Co., Inc., 1939.

1958

"Some Thoughts on Esthetic Research." *Journal of the A.I.A.*, December 1958, 40–41.

CREDITS

**Illustrations not credited below are from Frey's office files and personal papers.
Numbering refers to figure numbers within each chapter.**

courtesy The University of California at Santa Barbara Art Museum Architectural Drawing Collection:
A.2, A.4, A.5

R. M. Damora: 2.88, 2.89

courtesy Brad Dunning: Z.1, Z.2

courtesy Fondation Le Corbusier: 1.17, 1.20, letters on pages 13–17

Albert Frey (as photographer): 2.18–2.20, 2.23, 2.25, 2.44, 2.56, 2.64–2.66, 2.68–2.71, 2.72 (courtesy The A. Lawrence Kocher Papers, Special Collections, The Colonial Williamsburg Foundation Library), 2.73–2.75, 2.84, 2.86, 4.34

courtesy Mr. & Mrs. Sam Hinton: p. 59

Robin Noble: 4.11, 4.12, 4.30, 4.36, 4.37, 4.50–4.52

Joseph Rosa: 2.22

Palmer Shannon (courtesy The A. Lawrence Kocher Papers, Special Collections, The Colonial Williamsburg Foundation Library): 2.1–2.4, 2.29, 2.30, 2.32, 2.34

Julius Shulman: all cover images, A.3, 3.1, 3.2, 3.3, 3.5–3.9, 3.11, 3.13, 3.14, 3.16–3.24, 3.29, 3.30, 3.32, 3.34–3.39, 3.42–3.44, 3.46, 3.47, 3.49–3.51, 3.54, 3.56–3.64, 3.66–3.72, p. 105, 4.1–4.3, 4.5–4.9, 4.13, 4.14, 4.16, 4.18, 4.20, 4.21, 4.22, 4.25–4.27, 4.29, 4.31, 4.32, 4.38, 4.40–4.45

courtesy The A. Lawrence Kocher Papers, Special Collections, The Colonial Williamsburg Foundation Library:
2.12–2.17, 2.21, 2.31–2.38, 2.42, 2.43, 2.47, 2.50, 2.51, 2.59–2.61, 2.77

Stephen Willard: 2.76, 2.78–2.81, 2.82, 2.85

W. P. Woodcock: 3.55

FROM

Architectural Forum: 2.28
Architectural Forum (courtesy Museum of Modern Art Library, New York): 2.5
Architectural Record: 2.26, 2.27
Architectural Record (courtesy Museum of Modern Art Library, New York): 2.52–2.54, 2.83, 2.87
Architectural Record (courtesy Colonial Williamsburg Foundation Library): 2.45, 2.62, 2.63
Boesiger, Willy, ed. *Le Corbusier et Pierre Jeanneret Oeuvre Complète 1910–1929.* Zurich: Les Editions d'Architecture Artemis, 1964: 1.15, 1.16
Boesiger, ed. *Le Corbusier et Pierre Jeanneret Oeuvre Complète 1929–1934.* Zurich: Les Editions d'Architecture Artemis, 1964: 1.18, 1.22
Hubert, Christian, and Lindsay Stamm Shapiro. *William Lescaze.* New York: Institute for Architecture and Urban Studies / Rizzoli, 1982: 2.39–2.41
Rassegna: 1.5, 1.6, 2.84
Shelter: 2.10
Sunset: A.1
Yorke, F. R. S. *The Modern House.* London: The Architectural Press, 1934: 2.46

INDEX

Albert Frey: Modern Architect (exhibition), 137, 138
Allied Arts and Building Products Exhibition, N.Y., 23, 30
Allison and Rible, 61
Aluminaire House, 23, 24, 27, 29, 30, 32, 35, 51, 138; *25, 26, 28*
American Institute of Architects, 88
Amerika, 10
Architectural League Exhibition, N.Y., 23, 30
Architectural Graphic Standards, 47
Architectural Record, 21, 30, 35, 38, 42
Arter, A.J., 3

Bailey, Evera Van; see Purcell, William Gray
Banning Library, 103; *102*
Bauhaus, 4
Beatty, Hamilton, 24 (fn. 13)
Beaux Arts, 3, 21
Behrens, Peter, 23
Bel Vista, 87, 88
Benoist Guest House, 84, 87, 111; *85, 86*
Bourgeois, Victor, 4
Brandenstein Study, 53;
Breuer, Marcel. 61

Cahuilla Elementary School, 93; *92*
Campani, Frances, 30 (fn. 26), 138
Carey House, 112
Cathedral City Elementary School, 93
Chambers, Robson C., xi, 88, 107, 124, 125, 138
Clark, John Porter, xi, 51, 53, 54, 61, 62, 84, 88, 107, 115, 122, 137
Clauss, Alfred, 23, East Coast, n.5
Cody, William F., 137
Committee on Farmhouse Design of the President's Conference on Home Building and Home Ownership, 32
Concrete Parking Tower (project), 6
Cotton-Textile Institute, 38, 47
Cree House II, 111, 127; *110*

Dailey, Gardner, 137
Darien Guild Hall (project), 32, 37, 47
Davidson, J. R., 21, 51
Dellside Dairy (project), 74
Desert Hills Hotel (project), 111

Desert Hospital, 101; *100*
Downyflake Donuts Shop (project), 34
Dunning, Brad, 140
Dunning-Ford-Moore Cottage (project), 140; *139*

Eggericx, Jean-Jules and Raphael Verwilghen, 4, 5, 9, 10; *8*
Ellwood, Craig, 125, 137
Experimental Five Room House (project), 38, 112; *39*
Experimental Week-end House (project), 38, 42, 112

Factory of Steel and Glass (project), 5, 6
Farmhouse "A" (project), 32, 34, 37, 47; *33*
Farmhouse "B" (project), 32, 34, 37, 47; *33*
Farmhouse No. 6531 for U.S. Department of Agriculture (project), 41, 47
Farmhouse No. 6532 for U.S. Department of Agriculture (project), 41, 47
Ford, Tom, 140
Frey, Albert (father), 3
Frey, Hugo (uncle), 3
Frey, Ida (mother), 3
Frey House I, 62, 71; *63-67*
Frey House I with additions, x, 74, 77; *76, 78-83*
Frey House II, xi, 127, 132, 138, 140; *126, 128-131*

Gebhard, David, 77, 137
Goff, Bruce, x
Goodwin, Philip L., 51; with Edward Durell Stone, 53; with Louis C. Jaeger, 54
Gropius, Walter, 34, 61
Gruen, Victor, 125
Gut-Frey House, 41; *40*
Guthrie House, ix, 52

Halberg House, 52, 53
Harrison, Wallace K., 29
Hatton House, 68, 74
Hatton Guest House, 68, 74
Heineman, Arthur, x
Hitchcock, Henry-Russell, 30
Home Owners Loan Corporation, 61, 87
House of Prefabricated Walls and Roofs (project), 47
Housing for the Old (project-competition), 6
Howard, Ebenezer, 14
Huntington Historical Society, 30
Huntington Register of Historic Places, 30

In Search of a Living Architecture, ix, 54, 55-57
International Exhibition of Modern Architecture, MoMA, N.Y., 30
International Style: Architecture Since 1922, 30

Jaeger, Louis C. *See* Goodwin, Philip L.
Jeanneret, Pierre. *See* Le Corbusier
Johnson, Philip, 21 (fn .3); 30
Jones, A. Quincy, 111

Kappe, Ray, 137
Katherine Finchy Elementary School, xi, 94, 96; *95*
Kaufmann, Gordon, x
Kiesler, Frederick, x, 21
Kocher, A. Lawrence, ix, 9, 21, 23, 30, 32, 32, 35, 41, 42, 47, 51, 54; with Gerhard Ziegler, 21
Kocher Canvas Week-end House, 24, 38, 42, 51; *43-46*
Kocher, Dr. J. J., ix, 47
Kocher, Marge; East Coast, n.50
Kocher-Samson Building ix, 47, 49, 51, 89; *48, 50, 64, 65*
Koenig, Pierre, 137

Laszlo, Paul 125
Lautner, John x, 62, 127, 137
Le Corbusier x, 5, 6, 9, 10, 13, 14, 17, 23, 24, 32, 35, 41, 61, 75, 88, 135; with Pierre Jeanneret 9, 41, 107; Early Years, n.14-20, East Coast, n.13, 40
Lescaze, William, 21, 30, 35, 53, 54, 115
Leuenberger, Fluckiger, 5
Loewy House, 62, 69, 74; *70-73*
Loewy, Raymond, 69
Lynch, Michael, 30 (fn. 28)
Lyons House, 84

Maekawa, Kunio, 9, 10, 107
Markham House, 84, 112
May, Cliff, xi
McCoy, Esther, 23 (fn. 8), 137
Mendelsohn, Erich, 10, 124
Mies van der Rohe, Ludwig, 23
Miniature Golf Course (project), 38
Minimal Metal House (project), 6, 9, 42; *7*
Mirrored Pavilion, 133, 135; *134*
Modern Architecture, 30
Modern Architecture in California, MoMA, N.Y., 47

Mondrian, Piet, 41
Moore, Jim, 140
Muschenheim, William, 23
Muthesius, Hermann, 4

National Register of Historic Places, 30
Needles Unified School District, 76
Nelson House (project) and Store, 62
Nelson, Mary, 62
Neutra, Richard, ix, xi, 21, 23, 30, 47, 51, 61, 62, 88, 137
New York Institute of Technology, N.Y., 30 (fn. 26, 28)
New York State Department of Parks Recreation and Historic Preservation, 30 (fn. 27, 28)
Newton House (project) 132
North Shore Beach Estates (project), 118-119
North Shore Hotel, 118
North Shore Yacht Club, x, 77, 115, 118, 119; *116, 117*

Palm Springs Aerial Tramway, 122; *123*
Palm Springs City Hall, 107, 119; *108-109*
Palm Springs Desert Museum, 138, 140
Palm Springs Unified School District, 93
Pellietier House, 74; *75*
Pereira and Luckman, 125
Perriand, Charlotte, 9, 24
Première Apartments, 77, 112, 115; *113, 114*
Purcell, William Gray and Evera Van Bailey, ix, 53

Ralph-Barbarin House, 10, 35, 37; *36*
Real Estate Subdivision for Low-Cost Housing (project), 30, 32; *31*
Rice, Norman N., 24 (fn. 13)
Roth, Alfred 41, 9 (fn. 14), 41 (fn. 47)

Saint Michael's By-The-Sea, 119; *120, 121*
San Gorgonio Pass Memorial Hospital, 97, 101; *98, 99*
San Jacinto Hotel, 52, 112
Schiff House Addition, 125
Schiff Ranch House (project), 133
Schwarting, Jon Michael, 30 (fn. 26, 28), 138
Sert, José Luis, 9
Schindler, R. M., x, xi, 21, 47, 51, 53, 62, 137

Smoke Tree Ranch, 84, 133, 140
Stone, Edward Durell. *See* Goodwin, Philip L.
Subsistence Farmsteads (project), 10, 42
Sullivan, Louis, 53
Swaelmen, Louis van der, 5
Swiss Pavilion for 1939 World's Fair (project), 54

The American City, 11
Towards a New Architecture, 5, 32
Tramway Gas Station, 124, 138

United States Department of Agriculture, 41, 88

Van Pelt and Lind Architects, 51
Verwilghen, Raphael. *See* Eggericx Jean-Jules
Villa Hermosa, 87, 88, 112; *89-91*
Vista Colorado Elementary School, 96

Walker and Eisen, x
Wasmuth, 4
Weber, Kem, 21, 51
Webster, Erle and Adrian Wilson, ix
Weissman, Ernest, 9
Welton Becket, 125
Wendingen, 5
Werk, 4
Wie Baut Amerika? xi, 10
Williams, E. Stewart, 137
Williams, Williams, & Williams, 122
Wilson, Adrian. *See* Webster, Erle
Woolley House, 74; *72*
World War I and II, 4, 9; x, xi, 61, 87, 137
Wright, Frank Lloyd, 10, 74
Wright, Lloyd, x, xi, 53
Wurster, William, 47

Ziegler, Gerhard. *See* Kocher, A. Lawrence
Zimmerman, A. C., 47